DATING
WITHOUT
MATING

Revd Dr Jim Master

Dating Without Mating

Written and Compiled by Revd Dr Jim Master

Copyright ©2022 Jim Master

First published 2022

The right of Jim Master to be identified as the author of this work has been asserted by him in accordance with the Copyright, Designs and Patents Act 1988.

Published for Revd Dr Jim Master by Verite CM Ltd

All rights reserved. No part of this publication may be reproduced, stored in a retrieval system, or transmitted in any other form or by any means, electronic, mechanical, photocopying, recording or otherwise, without the prior permission of the author.

ISBN: 978-1-914388-28-6

Scripture quotations marked "NIV" taken from the Holy Bible,
New International Version (Anglicised edition). Copyright © 1979, 1984, 2011 Biblica. Used by permission of Hodder & Stoughton Ltd, an Hachette UK company.
All rights reserved.

'NIV' is a registered trademark of Biblica. UK trademark number 1448790.

Scripture quotations marked "NKJV" are taken from the New King James Version®. Copyright © 1982 by Thomas Nelson. Used by permission. All rights reserved.

Scripture quotations marked "NASB" are taken from the
NEW AMERICAN STANDARD BIBLE®, Copyright © 1960,1962,1963,1968,1971, 1972,1973,1975,1977,1995 by The Lockman Foundation. Used by permission.

Scripture quotations marked "KJV" are from The Authorised (King James) Version. Rights in the Authorised Version in the United Kingdom are vested in the Crown. Reproduced by permission of the Crown's patentee, Cambridge University Press.

Scripture quotations marked "ESV" are taken from the Holy Bible, English Standard Version (Anglicized). Published by HarperCollins Publishers © 2001 Crossway Bibles, a publishing ministry of Good News Publishers. Used by permission.
All rights reserved.

Printed in the UK by Verité CM Ltd

CONTENTS

Introduction 5

1. Would I marry this person? 7
2. What you feed on is what you become – flesh and spirit 11
3. How long do I date, before I get married? 15
4. Pornography, make a covenant with your eyes 19
5. Biblical understanding of types of categories of being single ... 25
6. How to pray to get yourself pure! 43
7. We are not homophobic 53
8. The sexual revolution and temptation 63
9. Biblical questions and answers 71
10. The danger of the media and what you watch 81
11. How to choose the right person to avoid
    later regrets or divorce 87

Conclusion 91

INTRODUCTION

One of the main problems today that Christians face is that we live in a world full of promiscuity. The frontline battle is "sexual warfare". To try to convince those Christians what is right and wrong between a male and female in their relationship there are two things: first, the strength of your relationship with Christ, and second, choosing the right partner for life.

Many Christians fall into the trap of thinking everything is okay in their relationship when they have become physical with their partner and yet Christ is being hurt at the same time. This book is to help young people stay on the right side of Christ, and not let them defile their bodies before marriage. It tries to unravel some issues that Christian believers should take biblically, and forms discussion questions on topics such as being single, marriage, who to choose as a partner, same-sex marriage, and courtship do's and don'ts.

Today, many go for the bronze and silver, but can't wait for the gold and fall short of the "Glory of God".

This book, written and compiled by Revd Jim Master, is practical as well as informative and is a tool that helps the individual to live the Christian life according to scripture.

CHAPTER 1

Would I marry this person?

Every Christian wants to get it right! The world has a saying: "There are plenty more fish in the sea." However, this should never be the thoughts of a Christian individual. When choosing a partner, you should be looking for a godly and upright person. Without prayer and patience, you so easily end up with the wrong person.

The Bible says, "To everything there is a season, a time to every purpose under the heaven" (Ecclesiastes 3:1 KJV). So, start by saying to yourself, "The person I agree to go out with, I should one day be prepared to marry." By praying and thinking along these lines, you will adjust your thought patterns into thinking, "I don't need a relationship with a few, but the one who God has chosen for me."

The reasons and purpose some Christians come under pressure: To be popular, peer pressure.

- To fill a previous break up.
- Need somebody in their lives to fill a gap.
- To try and have a physical relationship.
  However, the right reasons:
- You're looking at a life partner.
- You want to raise a family.

How do I find the right Christian partner?

The first thing is to share your feelings with a godly person who can pray with you for the right partner. I remember praying for a partner when I was 17 years old and met my wife seven days later. She was my first girlfriend and is still my wife after 36 years of marriage.

The Bible tells us, "And we know that in all things God works for the good of those who love him, who have been called according to his purpose" (Romans 8:28 NIV).

Some Christians will succumb to being asked out by an unbeliever, which makes things difficult in your Christian walk with Christ. You both will have completely different values and they will want a physical relationship with you. So, the best thing first is to invite them to church and then to Christ. Any other option will be a rollercoaster of unhappiness and pretence. There is nothing like having a relationship with someone who shares your Christian values and has a Christ-like understanding. We call this being equally yoked together.

> "Do not be unequally yoked together with unbelievers.
> For what fellowship has righteousness with lawlessness?
> And what communion has light with darkness?"
> (2 Corinthians 6:14 NKJV)

It is very tempting to been drawn into the world's thinking that we can withstand the temptation of the world. My experience has taught me different, that those who have been strong with the Lord, who have chosen an unbeliever as a partner, have sacrificed their faith in Jesus Christ for their partner.

However, those who have agreed to have a platonic relationship, with a view to bringing their friend to Christ, have seen great strides in building a pure relationship before marriage.

What are the guidelines to dating the right person and the questions that I should ask them?

1. Do you love Jesus enough to keep my life pure?

2. Are you willing to wait until we get married for a physical relationship?

3. Are you willing to pray with me through situations and discuss our problems?

4. Are you willing to be involved with me in church activities?

I believe if the answers to the above are all "yes!" then you have a good foundation for a pure Christian relationship. Anything less will only compromise your beliefs in Christ. As we look further into this course, we will learn some practical ways to attain this relationship.

As a Christian in dating relationships, we want to avoid hurting one another and dishonouring Christ by "defrauding" our brothers and sisters in Christ. I know someone who used to date continuously, not taking into consideration how many people they were hurting. Our Christian lives are built upon caring for one another and not playing around with people's lives. Jesus needs to be the centre of every relationship; if he's not then something else will be. As we get deeper into this subject, we find that having a relationship honouring to the Lord is the most wonderful and beautiful thing God ever created.

This is why a godly spouse is worth searching for and waiting for:

"He who finds a wife finds a good thing, and obtains favour from the Lord." (Proverbs 18:22 NKJV)

"House and wealth are an inheritance from fathers, but a prudent wife is from the Lord." (Proverbs 19:14

So, the person you go out with is the person you should be prepared to marry.

Discussion Questions

1. Am I willing to wait for the right Christian person to date?
2. Am I willing to spend time in prayer, outlining the right person?
3. Am I willing not to compromise my Christian beliefs for anyone?
4. When I meet someone am I willing to be friends first?
5. Once I met someone am I willing to keep physically pure?

CHAPTER 2

What you feed on is what you become – flesh and spirit

Today, many people are exposed to promiscuity and it attracts many Christians towards a society where they will go as far as they can physically before they call it a sin. It is natural to want to have a physical relationship with our partner and the world would see that this is normal. To be a virgin before you get married is a rarity; however, it is not insurmountable.

As we grow up into teenagers and adults our bodies change and hormones kick in. This is a natural progression for everyone and you don't need to be embarrassed about those feelings, but the key for Christian believers is to understand why we fight such issues and this can control us.

Paul the apostle speaks about this in Galatians 5:17 (NIV):

> "For the flesh desires what is contrary to the Spirit, and the Spirit what is contrary to the flesh. They are in conflict with each other, so that you are not to do whatever you want."

So, here we have the scenario where within ourselves there is a civil war. One part of you is saying "do it this way" and the other is saying "do it that way". It seems hard and difficult. The facts are "what we feed upon is what you will become". The exposure to various social media platforms has allowed many Christians to hide themselves away in a secret place to observe sexual acts without any accountability.

If you feed on sexually immoral material you will become sexually active. So, the answer then is to overt these things from your life. As the wages of sin is death, we have to find a form of discipline in not getting involved with any of these things that lead to a dead spiritual life.

How do I do that?

Ask yourself these questions:

- What am I watching on TV, social media, etc.? Is there bad language, sexual scenes?

- Am I going to night clubs that promote sexual fornication, excess drinking of alcohol, smoking, drugs and sexual music?

- Am I spending time alone with my partner causing temptation to succumb to sin?

- Am I using indecent language that promotes sexual acts?

- Am I going to parties that involve ungodly acts?

These are some of the things I should be steering away from and, instead, I should be feeding my spirit.

How do I do that?

- Getting involved with godly activities, such as serving in the local church.

- Spending every morning in pray asking the Lord to help you subdue the flesh and to increase the Holy Spirit in your life.

- Make sure you spend more time with godly people.

- Asking the Lord to develop your "ministry" and how to grow this, so your time is occupied on the things above.

- Pray for your "partner", that they will not tempt you into anything that is not of the Lord, keeping your relationship pure. Treat your partner like a sister or brother until you get married.

- Make your number-one goal to aim for a pure and great marriage.

All these things we should be aiming for as a priority in our relationship with our partner. If you have just become a Christian, all your sins can be wiped away and you can start again with godly practices. The Holy Spirit will help you change your life around and start living a Christian life. There are two paths, you can take. These roads are completely separate. It is no good trying to live on both paths. God will expose you and the consequences become untenable. So, don't lie to yourself and live a life of pretence.

This civil war in you can so easily be defeated by his Holy Spirit and your life can be wholesome, righteous and clean. Don't bow down to Satan's environment; look to Christ to feed your Spirit.

> "Brother and sisters, if someone is caught in sin, you who live by the Spirit should restore that person gently. But watch yourselves, or you also may be tempted." (Galatians 6:1 NIV)

Discussion Questions

1. Am I going to places that I shouldn't be going, such as nightclubs and certain parties?

2. What am I watching on television or social media? Does it have bad language, sexual acts?

3. What type of friends am I mixing with? Are they badly influencing my Christian life? Do I need to come away from them?

4. Am I spending time alone with my partner, allowing myself to fall into temptation? Who is the stronger spiritual partner?

5. Am I living a life of pretence, showing people that I am spiritual on Sundays, ministering, but involved with sexual acts, lies and all kinds of intentional sin?

CHAPTER 3

How long do I date, before I get married?

Dating is not a relationship that should stand still for too long.

> "And whatever you do, whether in word or deed, do it all in the name of the Lord Jesus, giving thanks to God the Father through him." (Colossians 3:17 NIV)

In some countries Christians don't date at all. Their lives are determined by information about their partners and conversations through social media. They still have a choice whether they marry the partner chosen by their parents and are not forced, but it seems to work really well.

In any relationship, there needs to be a romantic side that does not involve cause for temptation.

So, if the person you have chosen to date is going to be your lifelong partner. You should not allow yourself more than a year or you could end up in a sexual relationship. This determines the circumstances, such as two people living close by to each other. Of course, if you live geographically far apart, there is less cause for concern.

During courtship ask a few questions:

- Are we both Christians?

- Are we both bearing fruit that is evidence for our salvation? (Galatians 5:22-23)

- Are we both ready to fulfil the biblical roles of a husband and wife? (Ephesians 5:22-33)

* * *

As soon as you get engaged, go for premarital counselling with your pastor or spiritual leader.

If you know you are going to get married, get married sooner rather than later

If you don't know this is the person God has for you, then I would err on the side of caution and break it up before someone gets hurt. But if you are confident God wants you two to get married, then you can plan.

Your relationship is more important than your external circumstances, such as what house you live in or what cars you drive. If you can support yourselves and you are ready to fulfil the biblical roles in marriage, then I would get married if I were you. Even if things are not perfect, I believe you will cause yourself less damage by getting married.

Dating do's and don'ts!
Ten guidelines:

1. Don't be alone in the same room or house.

2. Date in places where there are lots of people, such as the cinema, restaurants or church.

3. Make sure there is no strong physical contact that leads to sexual acts.

4. Have respect for one another's bodies and don't cause the other one to sin.

5. Do spend time praying for each other with other people, such as parents and other couples.

6. Seek spiritual guidance continuously from mature Christians.

7. Make planning the wedding and honeymoon the primary goal to look forward to.

8. Enjoy the journey towards marriage by occupying your time with fun events.

9. Look forward to telling your children the Christian walk you had with your partner.

10. Don't be pressured by what the world thinks or says and let the Bible and Jesus be your focus.

Once you have these things in place the day of your marriage will be pleasing to the Lord.

> "So we make it our goal to please him, whether we are at home in the body or away from it." (2 Corinthians 5:9 NIV)

Date to marry and marry to date! All these things become pleasing to the Lord.

Discussion Questions

1. How many times a week do I see my partner?

2. Do we spend time alone when no one is looking?

3. Do we fall into getting too physical, almost leading to sexual contact?

4. Who is spiritually stronger to avoid any temptation?

5. How much time do I spend a week praying with my partner?

CHAPTER 4

Pornography, make a covenant with your eyes

> "I made a covenant with my eyes not to look lustfully at a young woman." (Job 31:1 NIV)

Most of the time we think sexual immorality starts from the heart. We feel, we think about it, and then we act according to it.

Sexual immorality doesn't start from the heart. The heart is just the second stage of sexual immorality.

Job knew about these stages of sexual immorality. He knew that it would always start from what he looked at. If he looked lustfully at a woman, the heart would start to think about that, and then push Job into sin.

Job made a covenant with his eyes never to look lustfully at women but, in contrast, David, who couldn't make that kind of covenant with his eyes, fell into sin.

There are many warnings about sexual immorality that have been given in the Bible, but it is something that is becoming hard for many people to avoid. And I can tell you that Christians are included.

Look at one of the warnings regarding sexual immorality in the Bible.

> "Whoever commits adultery with a woman lacks understanding.
> He who does so destroys his own soul." (Proverbs 6:32 NKJV)

You see, this is proof that not all sin is the same. Yes, ultimately all sin brings death, but they're not the same. You can't tell a lie and sin against your own body. You can't tell a lie and destroy your soul. But the Bible did not say a thief destroys his own soul or a liar destroys his own soul, but an adulterer destroys his own soul. There's something serious about sexual immorality that I believe we as humans don't fully comprehend.

> "'Whoever is simple, let him turn in here.' And for him who lacks understanding, she says to him, 'Stolen water is sweet, and bread eaten in secret is pleasant.'" (Proverbs 9:16-17 NKJV)

Here the lady is quoting a well-known saying which is a half-truth. And we all know that a half truth is a lie. In other words, what she is saying is the illicit sex of an adulterer is more satisfying than sex between a husband and wife, which God has sanctioned. Hence the saying, "Stolen water is sweet, and bread eaten in secret is pleasant."

And in all honesty, she is telling the truth, but she is not telling the whole truth because she does not tell you the end of the story.

Let's be honest. There is pleasure in sin; people don't commit sin because it hurts them. People commit sin because there is pleasure in it. There is an enjoyment in sin for a period of time and that pleasure in sin is what she is talking about. There is some genuine allure in the excitement, independence, camaraderie and pleasure in breaking God's command and counsel.

Sin has its pleasures for a season.

In the next verse in Proverbs, Solomon then tells the readers the part that she has conveniently missed out.

> "But he does not know that the dead are there, that her guests are in the depths of hell." (Proverbs 9:18 NKJV)

Sexual immorality is something that we should not play with.

A major area of sexual immorality that is in the church today is pornography. This is a serious issue in Christianity today. It is something we need to address in the church today. You will see many people don't look at the opposite sex yet lustfully they watch porn. Some people will preach against looking at the opposite sex lustfully but they cannot stop watching porn.

The problem that porn brings is not just addiction and sexual immorality. It is far beyond that. It affects one psychologically.

Upwards of 70 per cent of Christians or church members are still struggling with it today. And they watch at least once a month; 90 per cent of teens and 96 per cent of young adults are either encouraging, accepting or staying neutral on the discussion of this topic.

This is not a judgement of people struggling to get out of this addiction. But this is not something you should accept as part of your life. If Job says he has made a covenant with his eyes to not look lustfully on women, why should you not make the same covenant to not watch porn?

Many people don't even know how to relate with other people anymore because of this addiction. Many people are facing depression because they hate themselves for this. So, what happens in the unseen world when you watch pornography and it becomes an addiction? The plain and simple truth is that it becomes a stronghold, and once Satan has a stronghold in your life, he will not let go of it easily. This is why people want to stop but they can't for 10, 20, 30 years battling with this same sin. Why? Because it is a stronghold. One or two clicks and you have access to another world. And the more you are there in that world, the deeper the stronghold gets, and the more the claws wrap around you.

I remember a young man who went to my church and asked for prayer. He came to me saying, "Pastor, I need prayer." I asked him, "What for?" He said every time he would try to pray the images of the unholy things he was watching on the internet would pop up in his head. Anytime he would pray, he would begin to start seeing these things in his mind. And it would not stop. It was as if there was a literal wall between him and God. It even affected his relationship with God. This young man came to me in tears. He wanted it to stop, but it wouldn't.

There are so many people who are in the same situation. As soon as the young man said this to me, I thought of Isaiah 59:1-2 (NKJV):

> "Behold, the Lord's hand is not shortened, that it cannot save; nor His ear heavy, that it cannot hear. But your iniquities have separated you from your God; and your sins have hidden His face from you, so that He will not hear."

The problem with this stronghold is that it introduces other strongholds. Once pornography becomes a stronghold, lust becomes a stronghold, and that leads you to another stronghold, fornication, then graduates when you are married to adultery. One stronghold opens up the door to another – that is what happens to the unseen world when you watch pornography. It builds lust, and feeds it. It gives nutrition to lust. It gives lust everything it needs to grow.

When lust burns in the hearts of people, it causes them to behave foolishly and irrationally. The worst is that people will keep suffering for the irrational actions they commit through the lust of their hearts. Yet they will not stop from such actions.

The truth is, lust is something you have to fight at every stage of life. Even if you are 16 or 60 years of age, you have to fight lust. If you are single and you think lust will go away when you are married, that is a lie.

I believe one of the greatest regrets as humans is lust. If you want a better future for yourself, you have to deal with lust.

- Lust will cloud your judgement.

- Lust will destroy you.

- Lust will break up your home.

- Lust will destroy your health.

- Lust will take your money away.

- Lust will rob you of your joy.

- Lust will put a wall between you and God.

- Lust will throw you into a hole deeper than you ever thought you could go.

- Lust unchecked will leave you in a place where you will wonder how you got there.

I say all this because I have seen it first-hand with my own eyes. Lust does this to people.

I have seen lust and excessive masturbation and addiction to porn. People who had no intention of being with one another have to bring up a child together because of passion. I have seen people stay in relationships that were not leading to marriage because of lust.

Your ability to make good decisions goes out the window when lust is involved.

When you have sex on your mind your reasoning skills and your decision-making is poor. Lust makes you irresponsible. It is like a drug. When people are high on drugs, they are not as responsible as they would be with a sober mind.

Lust will make a man to forfeit and destroy a 20-year marriage for 10 minutes of pleasure. Isn't it really foolish for a man who has built a 20-year marriage to forfeit his wife and children and begin to pursue a girl for 10 minutes of pleasure? What is the wisdom behind a man leaving his wife behind to pursue another man's wife? Lust blindfolds a man and robs him of his wisdom and strength.

And one of the biggest lies you will hear is that lust is a male-only problem. No, women struggle with it just as much as men. There are some things people do that they try to hold the devil responsible for; meanwhile, it is their lust that caused them to act that way.

Why do you think Job made a covenant with his eyes? The term covenant is of Latin origin, meaning "a coming together". It presupposes two or more parties who come together to make a contract, agreeing on promises, stipulations, privileges and responsibilities. Job was in agreement with his eyes to know what he would look at.

Lust is not something to be played with.

> "And it came to pass, after the year was expired, at the time when kings go forth to battle, that David sent Joab, and his servants with him, and all Israel; and they destroyed the children of Ammon and besieged Rabbah. But David tarried still at Jerusalem. And it came to pass in an eveningtide, that David arose from off his bed, and walked upon the roof of the king's house: and from the roof he saw a woman washing herself; and the woman was very beautiful to look upon."
> (2 Samuel 11:1-2 KJV)

David seeing this woman led to all of his issues.

The eyes look and see. Then the heart will store up and the brain will start processing, giving you to think about it all the time.

When you commit sexual sin, you're not sinning against other people. You're not sinning outside of your body. You are not sinning to destroy other people's lives. But you are sinning against your body. You're destroying your own life.

Just to end with:

"Flee fornication. Every sin that a man doeth is without the body; but he that committeth fornication sinneth against his own body." (1 Corinthians 6:18 KJV)

Run from sexual sin and every form of sexual sin and make a covenant with your eyes.

Discussion Questions

1. Do you think that all sin is equal?
2. Do you think immorality has a higher price to pay?
3. Are you addicted to watching sexual acts intentionally?
4. Do you join in with friends who are unbelievers?
5. Do you get involved in sexual temptation, like parties, nightclubs, porn, etc.?
6. How do you control your sexual urges?
7. What do you do to overcome peer pressure?
8. Are you living one life as a Christian and another life as an unbeliever?
9. What are you doing intentionally to keep your life pure?
10. Do you have a mentor you are accountable to?

CHAPTER 5

Biblical understanding of types of categories of being single

Read 1 Corinthians 7:1-40.

"To the married I give this command (not I, but the Lord): a wife must not separate from her husband." (v.10 NIV)

Paul is saying, "I'm going to tell you something that doesn't come only from me, but it comes from the Lord." So he's referring back to the teaching of the Lord.

In verse 12, however, Paul says, "To the rest I say this (I, not the Lord): If any brother has a wife who is not a believer and she is willing to live with him, he must not divorce her" (NIV).

Now, as you work through these forty verses, the best way, I think, to do this is to understand that Paul is dealing with the Corinthian church. And in the Corinthian church, there were all kinds of issues, as you know, and marriage was one of them – marital status was a huge, huge issue. And apparently, as so often in the epistles of Paul, he is answering specific questions that have been brought up to him and he is trying to clarify things that the people need to know.

The background, however, of what he's doing here is the Corinthian chaos. People in the Corinthian church didn't come out of a Jewish background, so they didn't have an Old Testament view of marriage and divorce. They came out of paganism. They came out of godlessness and worldliness, and myriad marital problems and entanglements and misunderstandings existed.

For example, here would be a typical scenario that would exist in the Corinthian church with a whole group of converted Gentiles. Rome had no uniform marriage law. They would be under the influence of the Roman Empire. And the Empire contained, for example, many slaves, and many of the believers were slaves. A marriage in the strict and legal sense did not even exist for slaves. A master could allow what was called *contubernium* or, literally, "tent companionship" – living together, we would say. This was entered by slaves without a ceremony and could be ended if the master chose to end it, and at any point he could sell one of the slaves, and that would virtually end it anyway. It is like today's "live-in" sex partners.

As many early Christians were slaves, it is very likely that they had lived in such unions in the past and maybe in multiple unions and maybe were even still in such unions.

Now what? What's their status?

Beyond the slaves, for the common people, there was a custom called *usus*. It specified if a woman had dwelt with a man for a year, she was his wife. That would be what we call common-law marriage.

Another way of marrying for the common people was called *coemptio in manum*, "marriage by sale". You went to a man who was a little low on cash and you bought his daughter. This is a rather traditional way, kind of like the dowry. The father would sell his daughter to a man with money.

Now, if you get beyond the common people, you get to the upper classes and the noble people, a little more of the elite folks. They had marriage called *confarreation* which actually had a ceremony. The noble people had a joining of right hands. They said vows. They prayed prayers to Jupiter and to Juno. They had rings. (By the way, a little history about wedding rings which we find out about in Ancient Roman literature: somebody named Aulus Gellius cut up cadavers and said that there was a nerve that ran from the third finger on the left hand directly to the heart, and so the ring should be put on the third finger of the left hand. That was part of the ceremony.) They had wreaths, veils, flowers and cake, so guess where your modern wedding came from? An old Roman tradition picked up by the Roman Catholic Church and standardised.

The moral character of life in the Roman world and life around Corinth was low. Divorce was high where marriage existed. And with the slaves, where marriage really didn't exist, the changing of partners was a rather constant issue. And even the common people in their sort of informal covenants together broke them and went to other people.

So marriage in Paul's day was a disaster – like in our day – chaotic. And, of course, among the Corinthians that had come to Christ and been taught the standard of "one man, one woman" for life in a true covenant, a real covenant, a public covenant before God and before others, they had all kinds of questions, and the questions are the best way to break down this chapter.

Now, there are always those people who come up with the idea of no marriage, no sexual relationship at all. So the first question that we could sort of form as we jump into this chapter – and this must be behind what is going on as the chapter opens – is to ask the question: are normal physical relationships between a man and a woman somehow wrong? Are they unspiritual?

Let's start. Chapter 7:1, the apostle Paul says, "Now concerning the things of which you wrote to me" (NKJV). That's why we believe these are questions that need to be answered because Paul's referring directly to something that was written and sent to him. And you can imagine what was in that letter based upon the history that I just described to you, based upon the culture.

So first, "It is good for a man not to touch a woman" (NKJV). (That's a euphemism for sexual relationships!) It is good, it's okay. It's good not to have sexual relationships. That is to say, it's not evil. It falls within the realm of goodness, *kalos*: it's okay. Celibacy is all right. It's honourable, it's excellent. It's all right not to marry. It's all right to stay single.

But, verse 2: "Nevertheless, because of immorality, let each man have his own wife, and let each woman have her own husband." Why? Because of what? Immoralities.

You say, "I want to stay single all my life." Huh. Well, singleness is good if it is not the cause of sexual sin.

The general rule is: get married.

The reason is simple: because of temptation.

There is no place for fornication – that's the word translated here as "immoralities".

The fact of life is that if you try to stay single, as good as celibacy can be, marriage is the norm, and marriage is better if being single results in temptation.

I want you to know that Paul doesn't say get married because you've found somebody that you like. He says, really, get married because you're running at a very high risk of life if you don't.

There are six reasons for marriage.

1. Procreation (Genesis 1:28).

2. Pleasure (Hebrews 13:4).

3. Purity.

4. Provision. You take a wife in order that you might protect her and care for her and nourish her and cherish her as the Lord does the church.

5. Partnership. It's not good to be alone, you need a helper.

6. Picture. A picture of Christ in the church. But right in the middle of that is the notion of purity.

Each man is to have his own wife and each woman is to have her own husband. "The husband should fulfil his marital duty to his wife, and likewise the wife to her husband" (1 Corinthians 7:3 NIV).

Some people were saying, "Well, should we just stay single? Should we just be celibate? Should we see sex as evil?" Why would they say that? Because it mostly was in their world. Immorality was everywhere, fornication everywhere, adultery everywhere, all the time, by everybody. And so some were thinking they were taking the noble high ground and saying, you know, "Maybe we just don't do that at all," because it was a pornographic culture; it was a debased culture.

You know, it's nothing new for that to be the conclusion that people make in a time of debased living. I think there were many mediaeval monks who came to that conclusion, that the high ground was to be celibate. They were seeing sexual relationships of any kind in any relationship as some kind of a defilement.

But Paul says, "Look, it's okay to be single, it's okay to live without any relationships with the opposite sex, but it's a whole lot better to marry. And then when you do marry, you have a duty to fulfil to each other."

That duty, obviously, is to render the physical affection that is consistent and God ordained for the procreation and the pleasure of people in a marriage. In fact, the duty is so high in a marriage that the wife doesn't even have authority over her own body; the husband does. And likewise, the husband doesn't have authority over his own body, but the wife does.

So stop depriving one another.

Paul says that's not what God is asking. You look at the culture you live in and the history you come from in the past and maybe the high ground, the noble ground in this sex-saturated, sex-mad culture, is to just say, "I'll never do that, I'm going to live a life of complete abstinence, and this is the level of purity." Paul says, that's good, that's not wrong, that's not bad. But for most people, that's going to lead to immorality, so have your own wife, have your own husband, and fulfil your duties to each other, and do not deprive each other of that, unless by agreement for a time so that you may devote yourselves to prayer (v.5). But come together again. Why? So that Satan will not tempt you because of your lack of self-control. Don't do that. You will give Satan opportunity.

You think that you'll be purer by withholding that. But the opposite is true. The truth is you're going to go right down the path that Satan wants you to go, into sin, because you're going to be tempted because of your inability to exercise self-control.

Get married for the sake of purity, and when you're married, fulfil your marriage covenant physically. Do not deprive each other except for some great spiritual cause, and come back together again so that you don't put yourself in a position that Satan would tempt you because of your lack of self-control.

Now, Paul says in verse 6, "This I say by way of concession, not of command. Yet I wish that all men were even as I myself am. However, each man has his own gift from God, one in this way, and another in that" (NASB).

What he is saying is, "Look, celibacy is a gift. It's a gift. And I'm just conceding the fact, not commanding it. I can't command celibacy because that wouldn't be right. But I would, by way of concession, say, 'I wish you were like me,'" which is to say that he's not married.

Was he ever married? Most of us think he was because he was a member of the Sanhedrin, and you had to be married to be a member of the Sanhedrin. What happened to his wife? We don't know. We don't think he left her at home and took off for the rest of his life, so he probably lost his wife in death.

And this is what we talk about, the gift of singleness. And that is a gift.

> "I want you to be free from concern. One who is unmarried is concerned about the things of the Lord, how he may please the Lord, but one who is married is concerned about the things of the world, how he may please his wife, and his interests are divided." (vv.32-34 NASB)

So there are some benefits to being single, if you have been given the gift by God. Each man has his own gift. Celibacy is a gift. Remember the disciples in Matthew 19? The disciples said to Jesus (after his teaching on divorce), "It's better not to get married." And what did Jesus say? But not all men can handle that.

Not everybody can handle that.

It's okay. It's good. It's honourable. It has great potential to keep you single-minded and focused. But it's a gift – a unique gift.

The gift is best known by those who feel strong, complete comfort in being single and no strong desire for a partner, for an intimate partner, a life partner. It's an option. But please don't conclude that there's anything wrong with the God-given gift of physical intimacy. The last thing that God wants out of singleness is sexual promiscuity. Be single if that's not a problem. But if that's a problem, get married.

All right, the next question from the letter to Paul: "Should the formerly married remarry?"

And verse 8 is where he starts to talk about this, shifting gears, "But I say to the unmarried and to widows" – these would be two categories of formerly married people.

A widow is someone whose spouse died, right? Everybody knows that, it's universally understood. But who are unmarried people? Well, they can't be widows because it's the unmarried and the widows.

Now, there are only two ways that you can be married and then not be married. You either were widowed or you were divorced. That has to be what that means. So to those who have been divorced (called the "unmarried") and to widows, "it is good for them if they remain even as I".

The unmarried are the formerly married, the *agamos* – *gamos*, the married idea, and then *agamos*, the alpha privative, divorced people.

Verse 11: "If she leaves, she must remain unmarried, or else be reconciled to her husband" (NASB). Again, the same meaning has to be in view. Further on, in verse 34, you have the unmarried and the virgin. The unmarried aren't the widows and the unmarried aren't the virgins. So who are the unmarried? They have to be the people who were married and now are no longer married.

So formerly married people, now single by death, widows, or single by divorce, unmarried, what does Paul say? Well, it's good to be single, so it's good to stay single (v.8). It's good so that you can serve, so that you can be free as verses 32, 33 and 34 point out.

But look at verse 9. If they do not have self-control, let them what? Marry. "It's better to marry than to burn . . . " Not burn in hell but burn with desire.

It's fine. You were married, now you're single, be single, stay single, stay focused, live your life that way. That is preferable. I think that's great advice from the apostle Paul. But if you need to be married, if it's a problem physically, get married.

Let's remember that in 1 Timothy 5:14-15, the apostle Paul makes this very clear when he's talking about widows. He says, "I want younger widows to get married, bear children, keep house, and give the enemy no occasion for reproach; for some have already turned aside to follow Satan" (NASB).

You don't want a lot of young widows with all their desires being vulnerable to evil things around them. Stay single if you're able. Paul was able and he was focused; he was given that gift. It indicates that God can give that gift even after marriage if he so desires.

Be convinced that God has allowed your singleness for holy purposes. Pour your life into the kingdom. This is picked up in verses 26-27: "I think then that this is good in view of the present distress, that it is good for a man to remain as he is. Are you bound to a wife? Do not seek to be released. Are you released from a wife? Do not seek a wife." If you can handle that, it's good because it's tough in the world. The world they lived in was like the world we live in.

"But if you marry, you have not sinned; and if a virgin marries, she has not sinned" (v.28 NASB). They were asking those kinds of questions.

This abstinence idea had apparently taken over. It's okay to marry, it's okay to stay single. Yet when you do, you'll have trouble in this life, and I'm trying to spare you.

If you can be single, it simplifies your life. It narrows down the realm of your trouble. You've got enough trouble with yourself; you marry somebody, and now you've got two people, two sinners colliding. And you have a bunch of children, and you've got six sinners smashing into each other. And it just keeps going.

There's something to be said for just one sinner. It lowers the level of conflict. However, this assumes that one can deal with that kind of situation.

Paul even says,

> "The time has been shortened, so that from now on those who have wives should be as though they had none; and those who weep, as though they did not weep; and those who rejoice, as though they did not rejoice; and those who buy, as though they did not possess; and those who use the world, as though they did not make full use of it; for the form of this world is passing away." (vv.29-31 NASB)

Paul is saying, if you can stay single, it simplifies your life and you can pour your solo life into the kingdom, but you have to have the gift to do that or it just becomes a horrendous means of temptation.

So the question, then, is: is sexual activity unspiritual?

No. Singleness is good. Marriage is good, if you don't have the gift of singleness.

Should the formerly married remarry?

Yes, if they desire to be married because it's better to marry than to burn with passion. But if you can be single, be single and focus on the kingdom.

Another question is raised here: what are the alternatives for those who are married?

Now, understand what happens.

Maybe, let's say, a wife comes to hear the gospel. She believes in the gospel, she is saved, and now she's got an unconverted husband.

- Is she in a situation where she is unequally yoked together with an unbeliever?

- Is she having a relationship with a person who is part of the kingdom of Satan?
- Is this Christ with Belial, in the language of Paul in the 2 Corinthians letter?
- Is this light and darkness joined together?
- Is this sin and righteousness joined together?

Now you come to verse 12: "To the rest I say, not the Lord," – this is from me, the Lord hasn't got any instruction on this specifically – "if any brother has a wife who is an unbeliever, and she consents to live with him . . . " This is the opposite situation.

In this case, this is a brother who has a wife, and in this case she's the unbeliever but she wants to live with him. Should he divorce her just because she's an unbeliever? The answer: no, he must not divorce her.

"And a woman who has an unbelieving husband, and he consents to live with her, she must not send her husband away" (v.13 NASB), or divorce her husband.

Why?

"For the unbelieving husband is sanctified through his wife, and the unbelieving wife is sanctified through her believing husband; for otherwise your children are unclean, but now they are holy." (v.14 NASB)

What is that saying? It is saying, "Look, if your unbelieving partner loves you and wants to stay with you, you stay in that marriage." Why? Because you become the sanctifying instrument in the life of that nonbeliever and in the lives of the children of that union. You are the one receiving the grace of God that is being poured out on your life that will spill over to those unbelieving people and to your husband or your wife and your children.

Instead of the Christian being defiled by the unbeliever, the unbeliever is cleansed by the presence of the Christian.

We're not talking about salvation here, we're simply talking about the pure, wonderful blessings of God falling on a believer and spilling over to a nonbeliever and making a purer, cleaner, lovelier home.

God pours out his blessings on his redeemed and on the children of his redeemed. So it's the opposite of what they were thinking (I need to shake that partner because he's a pagan, he'll defile me). No, you'll be the means of a sanctifying influence on him.

However, verse 15 creates another scenario: "If the unbelieving one leaves, let him leave." Literally, if he takes himself out – that's the verb, if he eliminates himself, *chōrizō*, which is the technical term, really, for divorce – if an unbeliever divorces a believer, let him leave. "The brother or the sister is not under bondage in such cases, but God has called us to peace." Here is the second exception for divorce.

The first is adultery (we read about that in Matthew 19 and Matthew 5). The second is an unbeliever divorcing a believer.

You are not under bondage.

The bondage is broken, the bond is broken.

You are no longer bound.

"The married woman is bound by law to her husband while he is living; but if her husband dies, she is released from the law." (Romans 7:2 NASB)

Same language here. If an unbeliever leaves, you are not bound. What does that mean? The union has been broken, you no longer are bound by it, which then assumes that you have the right to remarry if a nonbeliever leaves because God has called us to peace, and the blessings of peace are what God wants for his children.

You say, "Well, I think I'll just hang on until the dying day. I think I'll fight this guy all the way to the end. I think I'll make it really impossible for him to divorce me because I want to see him saved." Good. However, verse 16 is written for you: "How do you know, O wife, whether you'll save your husband?" That's pretty practical, isn't it?

Marriage is not an evangelistic tool. It's an evangelistic context, but don't think that just by hanging on to this guy that somehow you're going to save him. How do you know whether you'll save him? Or how do you know, husband, whether you'll save your wife?

That's not the point. You have no knowledge of that.

When the unconverted person is determined to leave and seeks a divorce, you don't need to perpetuate the tension and the frustration and the hatred and the animosity under some notion that you might be the only person on the planet who can be the instrument of their salvation. That's for God to decide.

Well, the summary comes in verse 17, and this answers another question: should salvation change our marital status? That's kind of what we've been dealing with. "Only, as the Lord has assigned to each one, as God has called each, in this manner let him walk" (NASB).

Salvation doesn't really change anything. Now that you're a believer, you don't have to give up sex, throw out your partner; it doesn't change anything. Paul gives an illustration in verse 18: "Was any man called when he was already circumcised? He is not to become uncircumcised" (NASB). If you were saved when you were Jewish, you can stay that way. You don't become uncircumcised. If you were called in uncircumcision, don't be circumcised. Circumcision is nothing and uncircumcision is nothing, but what matters is the keeping of the commandments of God.

And that's simply an illustration to say everybody remains in the condition in which he was called.

So, if you were saved single, that doesn't change.

If you were saved married, that doesn't change.

If you were saved and suddenly, your unconverted spouse wants to divorce you, stay the way you are.

> "Were you called while a slave? Do not worry about it; but if you are able also to become free, rather do that. For he who was called in the Lord while a slave, is the Lord's freedman; likewise, he who was called while free is Christ's slave. You were bought with a price, do not become slaves of men. Brethren, each one is to remain with God in that condition in which he was called." (vv.21-24 NASB)

So how does that work out?

BIBLICAL UNDERSTANDING OF TYPES OF CATEGORIES OF BEING SINGLE

You come, you receive the Lord Jesus Christ, you're a converted husband, you have an unsaved wife.

You're a converted wife, you have an unsaved husband.

What are you supposed to do? Withhold from him a physical relationship? Divorce him?

Throw him out of the house?

No, stay where you are. Stay where you are.

You're single and you come to Christ. Are you now supposed to be a monk the rest of your life? Are you supposed to be celibate the rest of your life?

No. If you have that gift, fine. If you don't, get married.

Single or married, whatever God wills in whatever situation you're in, stay that way. This is so important because Christianity was never intended to just rip and shred families; the very opposite is true. And unless that unbeliever wants to leave, you become the sanctifying influence for the one that stays.

So, is our sexual relationship somehow unspiritual? No.

Should those saved after they're widowed or divorced remarry? Yes, you have the freedom to remarry or stay single, whatever is God's will for you.

What are the alternatives, then, for married people, to Christians? No divorce. And if you do leave, you don't remarry anybody else and you come back to your husband. Those are your two options. If you're married to a non-Christian, the non-Christian decides to divorce you, let it happen. You're free to remarry.

Now, there's another question in Paul's mind at this point. Verse 25: "Now concerning virgins . . . " – these are the never married. We've dealt with the single and the married and the widowed and the formerly married, divorced, and now we get around to the virgins.

Now, this is probably what was going on – get the big picture. They've got this sexually perverted culture, they want to distance themselves from the world, and so they come to the conclusion that if they just distance themselves completely from physical relationships, this is going to be the spiritual high ground. Therefore, there would be people who had never been married – men and women – virgins would cover men and women who'd never married. They'd never known a man, to borrow the biblical euphemism. *Parthenoi*. It is used in Revelation 14:4 one time to refer to men. That's why I say, it can be men or women, although most often it refers to women. These are people who had never had a relationship.

What do they do? Do they just stay that way?

"Now concerning virgins, I have no command of the Lord." The Lord didn't say anything. However, Paul says that he will give his opinion literally "as one who by the mercy of the Lord is trustworthy". He is saying, "I will give you a faithful judgement as one who is trustworthy" because he is inspired by the Lord. In verse 26 he says, "I think then that this is good, in view of the present distress, that it is good for a man to remain as he is" (NASB).

They were, by the way, about seventeen years from the first general persecution under Domitian, the sixth emperor of Rome, and it was a massacre and a bloodletting of Christians. So he's saying, look, if you're single and you've never been married, so you're not now married to a believer or non-believer, you're not divorced, you're not widowed, you're in the category of never having been married, boy, that's a good place to be in. That's a good place because of the present distress, the challenges that are coming on us. It's going to be a tough world. A few years from now, some of you are going to be killed. Diocletian's persecution stretched across the Roman world. But in verse 28 we read, "If you marry, you have not sinned; and if a virgin marries, she has not sinned" (NASB).

Are you beginning to get the picture of what they were asking him? That singleness seems to be the right thing. No sexual relationship seems to be the right thing. And he's setting all that aside.

Look, there's trouble in the world, singleness is great because you're not going to bring a family into the world and then watch your children being burned at the stake. There's something to be said for being single in a time of terrible, frightening persecution. But if you marry, you haven't sinned. And if a virgin marries, she hasn't sinned. "Yet such will have trouble in this life, and I'm trying to spare you."

And then he says: "Look, it's a short time, life, it's a short time. For some of you, it's a very short time because you're going to get caught in persecution. So, from now on, those who have wives should be as though they had none. Those who weep as though they didn't weep, and those who rejoice as though they didn't rejoice, and those who buy as though they didn't possess, and those who use the world as though they didn't make full use of it, for the form of this world is passing away" (see vv.29-31).

Marriage has no relation to the eternal, right? You remember when they said to Jesus, "Whose wife shall she be in heaven?" And Jesus said, "In heaven, there is neither marrying nor giving in marriage" (see Matthew 22:23-30).

This is good advice. Paul says the pressure of the system, the problems of the flesh, living in this life, and the passing of the world means that if you can concentrate on the eternal things in dire times, you simplify your life.

We're all going to have to simplify. We're all going to have to pull things in. We're all going to have to live in these difficult, difficult times. But for single people, life is simpler and not nearly as threatening or painful.

In verse 32-33, he adds, "I want you to be free from concern. One who is unmarried is concerned about the things of the Lord, how he may please the Lord; but one who is married is concerned about the things of the world, how he may please his wife." And that's exactly what he ought to be concerned about.

Married folks have divided preoccupations, divided responsibility. "His interests are divided. The woman who is unmarried and the virgin is concerned about the things of the Lord, that she may be holy both in body and spirit; but one who is married is concerned about the things of the world, how she may please her husband" (v.34 NASB).

And that's exactly what she ought to be concerned about.

And "the things of the world" – this doesn't mean sinful things, it just means the issues of life. "I say this for your benefit; not to put a restraint on you, but to promote what is appropriate and to secure undistracted devotion to the Lord" (v.35 NASB). You know, Paul was living this as a single man who had once been married, and he understood the single focus of this. He advises these virgins in the same way that he advised the formerly married in this passage and says, "Stay where you are. If you're married, stay married. If you're single and you can do it, stay single. And if you're a virgin and you can deal with that, stay that way."

So the bottom line here, up to this point, is that becoming a Christian does not of necessity mean that you have to make some dramatic alteration of your marital status. That's not what the Lord requires.

Two more questions remain here.

Should fathers spare their daughters the difficulties of marriage and keep them virgins for life? Oh boy, some really well-intentioned fathers were saying, "Well, I don't want you marrying some of the men in the world out there. I don't want to have you deal with all of that, all the immorality that may have been a part of their lives in the past." You can understand this. A father comes to Christ, the father's in the church, he's got young daughters that are coming up. There are other men in the church. There are the young men in the church, single men in the church, but their lives before Christ have been very sinful lives. And this Christian father says to his daughters that he's raising them in the things of Christ. "I don't want you to get married. I don't want you to do that. I want you to be pure. I want you to be devoted to Christ. I want you to be focused on the life of the church. I'll take care of you, as your father. I'll care for your life. You can stay at home and you can spend your life in the service of the Lord and honouring the Lord."

So, apparently, some of these fathers thought this was really a great idea.

Paul needs to answer that.

> "If any man thinks he is acting unbecomingly toward his virgin daughter, if she is past her youth and if it must be so, let him do what he wishes, he does not sin; let her marry." (v. 36 NASB)

You know what had happened? Some fathers were making a promise. "I'm going to keep you a virgin. I'm going to protect you from this wicked, sinful world. I'm going to protect you from these men. I'm not going to put you in a position to be married and deal with all the troubles of life. I'm going to take care of you."

And then the girl gets older, she comes into maturity, she's past her childhood, and she wants to get married. And he's kind of stuck and he's saying, "Well, what do I do?" He now thinks he's acting unbecomingly towards his daughter. She doesn't want this.

So Paul says, "Let her marry." But, on the other hand, in verse 37 he says, "He who stands firm in his heart, being under no constraint, but has authority over his own will, and has decided this in his own heart to keep his own virgin daughter, he will do well" (NASB).

Discussion Questions

1. Is being single and celibate a gift?
2. How long have you been single and are you praying for a partner?
3. Has God spoken to you about a partner?
4. What do you look for in a man or woman?
5. Are you willing to wait for the right person?

CHAPTER 6

How to pray to get yourself pure!

You know, you talk to God and many of your prayers go unanswered.

Have you asked yourself this question: is there anything in my life that is stopping my prayers being answered and causing God to ignore me?

Have you ever thought about this?

Have you thought about the God to whom you are making your prayers?

Many people pray and they expect God to answer their prayers and, somehow, they don't get answered, so they give up praying and say it's not real and the Bible is not really true. The Bible is very true from the beginning to the very end.

I want you to read this chapter carefully, because it just may be that you will discover one of the reasons why your prayers don't get answered.

> "It was about this time that King Herod arrested some who belonged to the church, intending to persecute them. He had James, the brother of John, put to death with the sword. When he saw that this met with approval among the Jews, he proceeded to seize Peter also. This happened during the Festival of Unleavened Bread. After arresting him, he put him in prison, handing him over to be guarded by four squads of four soldiers each. Herod intended to bring him out for public trial after the Passover.
>
> "So Peter was kept in prison, but the church was earnestly praying to God for him.

> "The night before Herod was to bring him to trial, Peter was sleeping between two soldiers, bound with two chains, and sentries stood guard at the entrance. Suddenly an angel of the Lord appeared and a light shone in the cell. He struck Peter on the side and woke him up. 'Quick, get up!' he said, and the chains fell off Peter's wrists.
>
> "Then the angel said to him, 'Put on your clothes and sandals.' And Peter did so. 'Wrap your cloak around you and follow me,' the angel told him. Peter followed him out of the prison, but he had no idea that what the angel was doing was really happening; he thought he was seeing a vision. They passed the first and second guards and came to the iron gate leading to the city. It opened for them by itself, and they went through it. When they had walked the length of one street, suddenly the angel left him.
>
> "Then Peter came to himself and said, 'Now I know without a doubt that the Lord has sent his angel and rescued me from Herod's clutches and from everything the Jewish people were hoping would happen.'" (Acts 12:1-11 NIV)

The scripture says about that time King Herod laid hands on some who belonged to the church in order to mistreat them. He had James the brother of John put to death with a sword. And when he saw that it pleased the Jews he proceeded to arrest Peter too. Now it was during the Festival of Unleavened Bread, after the Passover, and when he had seized Peter, he put him in prison, delivering him to four squads of soldiers. Four squads would be sixteen soldiers. They were there to guard him, and to bring him out before the people.

Peter was kept in the prison. But prayer was *being made fervently* by the church to God. Would you say that you pray fervently? Or do you say, "I just prayed." Well, let's look at what's going on right here and maybe discover something about our own prayer life.

So Herod, he had James killed and that seemed to satisfy the Jews who hated the Christians. As that seemed to work, he had Peter arrested, put in prison, and it's very evident that Herod intended to kill him – that he intended to bring him out before the people and kill him with a sword, as he did James, and he figured that the Jews would be satisfied by Christians being killed. The result is that the Christians gathered together, the Scripture says in Mary's house, and there they gathered together to pray for Peter. They remember, probably, that James was killed without any warning. So here's Peter, their leader who they know is going to be killed, and so they're praying but they have to be struggling to some degree because they know how a prisoner is imprisoned by the Romans. And so they're praying and praying for God to release him.

How many times have cell phones not been answered because of bad reception? How many know that there are certain places that you can go that the cell phone don't work? Sometimes we find ourselves talking to God about issues in our lives but God doesn't answer and we wonder whether or not God can hear us.

Why is God is not answering your prayers?

As a matter of fact, there are several reasons why prayer does not get answered, and I'll give seven reasons why God won't answer your prayers. You may ask yourself, what has this got to do with dating? Well, you find out the more you pray the more you overcome the power of the flesh.

I want God to answer my prayers – no, I *need* God to answer my prayers. And God wants to answer your prayers. It's not that God is ducking and dodging you. It's not that he doesn't want to answer your prayer. God wants to answer your prayers.

But the Bible clearly gives us instructions on reasons why God won't answer prayer.

Let's look at the seven reasons. I want you to examine your life and see if any of these might be the reasons why God's not answering your prayers.

Here's what God says:

> "Call to Me, and I will answer you, and show you great and mighty things, which you do not know." (Jeremiah 33:3 NKJV)

So the question is, how come your prayers aren't being answered?

Reason Number 1: Things you do

> "Surely the arm of the Lord is not too short to save, nor his ear too dull to hear. But your iniquities have separated you from your God; your sins have hidden his face from you, so that he will not hear. For your hands are stained with blood, your fingers with guilt. Your lips have spoken falsely, and your tongue mutters wicked things." (Isaiah 59:1-3 NIV)

What's the difference between your iniquities and your sins?

Sin means you just missed the mark; you did what you shouldn't have done.

Your *iniquities* are *wickedness* (Greek: *aven*). It means not only did you sin but you planned to sin, it was premeditated sin, you orchestrated it, you wanted it so you made it happen.

It is one thing to fall in to sin unintentionally, but another thing to know it, and premeditate it. God's reaction is Isaiah 59:2 "so that he will not hear".

> "For though the righteous fall seven times, they rise again, but the wicked stumble when calamity strikes." (Proverbs 24:16 NIV)

It is when you are walking through life and trip up and fall and stay there, lie down in the mud, move in, pay rent. You practise it, you buy into plans. You subscribe to it. That's *iniquity.* That's enabling. God says when you bought into sin, you accepted and moved in. When the person is wicked, God says it is difficult for him to answer your prayer.

Paying more money into something that is sinful than you give in tithes and offerings, when you purposely planned it and it's premeditated, when you have accepted this lifestyle, that makes it extremely difficult for God to hear and respond.

Reason Number 2: Things you think

> "If I had cherished sin in my heart, the Lord would not have listened; but God has surely listened and has heard my prayer. Praise be to God." (Psalm 66:18-20 NIV)

Psalm 66:18 in the KJV says, "If I regard iniquity in my heart, the Lord will not hear me."

If I regard iniquity in my *heart* – it has to do with my *thinking!* In Hebrew that word "regard" means if I can see it, if I can imagine it, if I can picture it. And the word "heart" means your thoughts and your feelings. So this verse is saying that if I can see a picture of sin in my mind, if I can feel it in my heart, then God will not hear me when I pray.

That's an important thing because some have gone around *thinking* and *feeling* that as long as they don't do it, they're okay. We can dream about it and ponder it and peer at it from every side and imagine it and we're okay as long as we don't do it. But Psalm 66:18 says it *does matter.* The scripture says if I picture it in my mind, and if I can feel it in my *heart*, it makes it *difficult for God to respond* to my prayer.

We want to live a life that God answers our prayers, and I'm going to tell you something: there's nothing like *living a life when God answers your prayer.* Nothing can compete.

What's even greater is that you live the kind of life where you don't even have to utter the prayer. God answers your prayers before you even ask them. That is my experience in my walk with God.

This is what is important. God wants to answer your prayer. He wants to show you great and mighty things according to scripture:

> "For the eyes of the Lord range throughout the earth to strengthen those whose hearts are fully committed to him. You have done a foolish thing, and from now on you will be at war." (2 Chronicles 16:9 NIV)

When we learn about what it is that causes him to not hear our prayers, it's telling us that what God wants us to do is *take control of our thought life.* You've got to take control of your thought life. Taking control of what you think, not just what you do, is important to God.

Let me not think that I can just think about anything.

Thoughts might come to your mind but you don't have to let the thought land. You don't have to let the bird come in and lay eggs.

> "Casting down arguments and every high thing that exalts itself against the knowledge of God, bringing every thought into captivity to the obedience of Christ." (2 Corinthians 10:5 NKJV)

And any thought that doesn't agree with God, what's in God's Word, is not real for your life. Capture that thought in season because here's what happens. When you sow a thought, when you accept a thought:

- you sow a feeling.
- you reap an act.
- you reap a habit.
- you reap a lifestyle.
- you reap a destiny.

Let's be clear: if you keep on living your life a certain kind of way, you will not be called a child of God.

So, it's not only what you do, but what you think.

Reason Number 3: The motive behind it

> "You ask and do not receive, because you ask amiss, that you may spend it on your pleasures." (James 4:3 NKJV)

God says that you ask and he doesn't give it to you because you asked him for a worthless reason. You're asking for something that's not good, and only beneficial to you. Therefore, God says he can't answer what you ask. You ask it for your own pleasures. It's not about the kingdom. It's not about advancing God's kingdom. It's about you.

You asked him for a car but you didn't pick up anybody and bring them to church. They need him too. He gave you a new house but you aren't making room for anybody, no homeless person. You just want it so you can brag to your friends about your new house.

Reason Number 4: According to his will

> "This is the confidence we have in approaching God: that if we ask anything according to his will, he hears us. And if we know that he hears us – whatever we ask – we know that we have what we asked of him." (1 John 5:14-15 NIV)

In other words, God is saying, ask and he'll answer you, if what you ask is according to his will. This means that the reason he may not be answering you is because what you're asking him is not according to his will.

Let me help you out for a second.

There's no need to ask God to give you the numbers on the Lottery; that is not according to his will.

There's no need to ask God to get a divorce so you can hurry up and marry someone else; that's not according to his will.

If you pray according to the will of God and you're in love with his will, the scriptures say that we can know that he hears us. Let's be assured that this God is not playing hide-and-seek, trying to hide; he's not trying to duck and dodge. He wants to manifest himself to you. And the best thing we can do is examine ourselves and find out why he's not responsive to our prayers.

Reason Number 5: Marital conflict

> "Husbands, in the same way be considerate as you live with your wives, and treat them with respect as the weaker partner and as heirs with you of the gracious gift of life, so that nothing will hinder your prayers." (1 Peter 3:7 NIV)

If God's going to keep on answering prayers, *respect your wife*.

I had to learn to engage in my wife's world.

I had to learn to feel what she was feeling and be compassionate.

I had to learn to be sensitive because I wanted God to answer my prayer.

I had to enter into her world. I had to go shopping with her. I had to watch her programmes on television. I had to read the books that she's read.

Reason Number 6: Unbelief

> "When they came to the crowd, a man approached Jesus and knelt before him. 'Lord, have mercy on my son,' he said. 'He has seizures and is suffering greatly. He often falls into the fire or into the water. I brought him to your disciples, but they could not heal him.' 'You unbelieving and perverse generation,' Jesus replied, 'how long shall I stay with you? How long shall I put up with you? Bring the boy here to me.' Jesus rebuked the demon, and it came out of the boy, and he was healed at that moment. Then the disciples came to Jesus in private and asked, 'Why couldn't we drive it out?' He replied, 'Because you have so little faith. Truly I tell you, if you have faith as small as a mustard seed, you can say to this mountain, "Move from here to there," and it will move. Nothing will be impossible for you.'" (Matthew 17:14-20 NIV)

When the disciples asked Jesus why they could not cast out the demon, Jesus said to them that it was because of their *unbelief*. When you come to God, you've got to believe that he can do it. The reason he doesn't answer is because you don't believe; you doubt.

> "And without faith it is impossible to please God, because anyone who comes to him must believe that he exists and that he rewards those who earnestly seek him." (Hebrews 11:6 NIV)

It says when you come to God, you must first believe in him, and that he rewards every one of them that diligently seeks him.

You have to believe. You have to come to God and believe he's going to answer your prayer.

You've got to believe he's a burden-bearer, heart-regulator, mind-fixer.

You've got to believe he's a healer.

You've got to believe money will be put in your bank.

You've got to believe your bills will be paid.

You've got to believe that he can answer your prayers.

Without faith it's impossible to believe; impossible to please God.

Reason Number 7: Obedience

> "If anyone turns a deaf ear to my instruction, even their prayers are detestable." (Proverbs 28:9 NIV)

God wants to orchestrate your life, to call the shots in your life. If you call your own shots and you don't even recall what the Word says, then the Bible says your "prayers are detestable", an abomination to God. If you don't use the Word to guide and orchestrate your decisions, God can't answer your prayers because you don't give any credence to the scriptures in the decisions that you make in your life. And that's why your life is a mess.

Discussion Questions

Discuss the seven points that prevent answered prayer:

1. Things you do

2. Things you think

3. The motive behind it

4. According to his will

5. Marital conflict

6. Unbelief

7. Obedience

CHAPTER 7

We are not homophobic

How to deal with people who believe in same-sex marriage
This is a very important subject for many Christians whose beliefs are contrary to what society believes. The Bible tells us, clearly, about certain subject, like premarital sex, immorality and same-sex couples. But in all these circumstances, we should never allow ourselves to fall into hating anyone, but to love always, despite our beliefs. Our treatment should be equal in terms of the human being and we should never treat anyone with contempt. However, I would like to share an approach, and breakdown some of the history of where this all started.

It is very likely that the subject of same-sex relationships is one to which many will listen with different ears.

What I want to do first of all is to approach it philosophically, to set the scene, and then I want us to come to scripture, and see what the Bible has to say. Then I want to work through the practical implications of this, because my purpose is not just to be theological but to be pastoral.

I want to talk about four things.

1. I want to talk briefly about the society of which we are a part and understand the context in which we live.

2. Then we'll talk about the scripture to which you must submit.

3. Then the struggle with which some of us live.

4. Then we will talk about the strategy by which I'm going to propose that we live.

Number 1
History
Let me talk first about the society of which we are a part. There has been a radical change in the collective cultural consciousness and conscience regarding same-sex relationships in recent decades.

Society
Fifty years ago, homosexuality was illegal in most countries of the world. But the repealing of those laws and the consenting act between adults was like a fall of dominos in the UK and around the world.

The Buggery Act of 1533, passed by parliament during the reign of Henry VIII, is the first time in law that male homosexuality was targeted for persecution in the UK. Completely outlawing sodomy in Britain – and by extension what would become the entire British Empire – convictions were punishable by death.

It was not until 1861 with the passing of the Offences Against the Person Act, that the death penalty was abolished for acts of sodomy – instead being made punishable by a minimum of ten years imprisonment.

The Criminal Law Amendment Act 1885, however, went a step further, once again making *any* male homosexual act illegal – whether or not a witness was present – meaning that even acts committed in private could be prosecuted. Often a letter expressing terms of affection between two men was all that was required to bring a prosecution.

The legislation was so ambiguously worded that it became known as the "Blackmailer's Charter", and in 1895, Oscar Wilde fell victim.

The Report of the Departmental Committee on Homosexual Offences and Prostitution, better known as the Wolfenden Report, was published in 1957, three years after the committee first met in September 1954. It was commissioned in response to evidence that homosexuality could not legitimately be regarded as a disease and aimed to bring about change in the current law by making recommendations to the government. Central to the report findings was that the state should focus on protecting the public, rather than scrutinising people's private lives.

It took ten years for the government to implement the Wolfenden Report's recommendations in the Sexual Offences Act 1967. Backed by the Church of England and the House of Lords, the Sexual Offences Act partially legalised same-sex acts in the UK conducted in private between men over the age of 21.

Scotland and Northern Ireland followed suit over a decade later, in 1980 and 1981 respectively. The Sexual Offences Act represented a stepping stone towards equality, but there was still a long way to go.

In 1966 The Beaumont Society was set up to provide information and education to the general public, medical and legal professions on "transvestism", and encourage research aimed at a fuller understanding. The organisation is now the UK's largest and longest running support group for transgender people and their families.

In the wake of the Stonewall Riots in New York in June 1969 over the treatment of the LGBT community by the police, the UK Gay Liberation Front was founded (GLF) in 1970. The GLF fought for the rights of LGBT people, urging them to question the mainstream institutions in UK society which led to their oppression. The GLF protested in solidarity with other oppressed groups and organised the very first Pride march in 1972, which is now an annual event.

To most of our society this move is deemed to be good and just and right and fair.

That in itself raises an intriguing question. How has something that was universally criminalised fifty years ago, in such a short time become universally not only accepted but affirmed and even promoted, as it is today in our schools? You know, we're not as free as we think we are. All of us become victims of the environment in which we live and its worldview, complete with its blinkers and its blind spots, because it always has its blinkers, it always has its blind spots. It's easy for us to see the blind spots of modernism, as in, let's say, things like racism. But we have our own blind spots as well.

Another value, of course, of "post modernism" is "political correctness". And I suggest that is because there aren't any rules governing values, which is like building on sand: you try to build and everything begins to move, so don't challenge it; that's uncomfortable. Let's have an assumed consensus that certain things just "are" and don't challenge them – our nation in the UK is extremely politically correct and our media is totally predictable. What kind of discussions will they have on some of these kinds of issues, because there's this agreement that there's certain things that are sacrosanct and we shouldn't challenge them.

This makes it hard for Christians to speak of their beliefs or give a biblically-based opinion. Yet we are supposed to have free speech. However, it is possible to have free speech without "inciting hatred" towards our fellow human beings. We can give a reason for our beliefs without any animosity, and agree to disagree, without being prejudiced.

That's the society of which we are a part today.

Number 2

In light of that, let me turn now to my second area, which is the Scripture to which we must submit. And if we are Christian people, then of course the scriptures are not just guidelines, they represent truth.

And we're dealing here not with reason alone (though they are reasonable); not with values alone (though they certainly show us values). We are dealing with Revelation. By that we mean God is revealing what otherwise we may not know, and speaking into all cultures, of all times, to all generations.

That does not mean that the writers are influenced by the culture of that day and the society of the day because, of course, they were writing initially into that context, and we have to do the hard work of understanding something about the cultural context that the scriptures were being written in.

Revelation primarily centres on the moral character of God as the supreme revelation of scripture is to us. God has never changed his mind on any moral view in scripture. If he did, then Jesus dying on the cross would have been wasted.

Now, let me just take a few moments to give you the biblical passages on homosexuality, and they are very few; there's only four main scriptures.

In the city of Sodom, in Genesis 19, there was a group of homosexual men who wanted to rape two men who were guests of Lot, who was living in Sodom.

The issue here is not about homosexual orientation but sexual violence and homosexual rape. In fact, the word "sodomy" in the English dictionary comes from this event in Sodom: sodomy is buggery. It is male homosexual relationship, or part of it.

This event is referred to twice in the New Testament: "[Lot], who was distressed by the depraved conduct of the lawless" (2 Peter 2:7 NIV) and "Sodom and Gomorrah and the surrounding towns gave themselves up to sexual immorality and perversion" (Jude 1:7 NIV).

In Leviticus chapter 18 where there's a catalogue of sexual prohibitions, it says, "Do not have sexual relations with a man as one does with a woman; that is detestable" (Leviticus 18:22 NIV).

In the New Testament, in Romans 1:26, Paul speaks of homosexual acts. Regarding women he says, "Even their women exchanged natural sexual relations for unnatural ones" (NIV), and it's clearly speaking about lesbian activity there. And verse 27 speaks of men in the same way: "The men also abandon natural relations with women and were inflamed with lust for one another" (NIV).

Let me give you a final reference:

> "**Do not be deceived. Neither the sexually immoral nor idolaters nor adulterers nor men who have sex with men nor thieves nor the greedy nor drunkards nor slanderers nor swindlers will inherit the kingdom of God.**" (1 Corinthians 6:9-10 NIV)

It is a long list of people who he says are not going to inherit the kingdom of God.

But the next verse is a great verse:

"You were washed, you were sanctified, you were justified in the name of the Lord Jesus Christ and by the Spirit of our God." (1 Corinthians 6:11 NIV)

What we must conclude from those references is, the Bible says nothing about "homosexual orientation" (that is the attraction that one person may have for somebody of their own gender) but that it is consistently hostile to "homosexual acts". (Incidentally, it is also hostile to heterosexual acts outside of marriage.) Nowhere in Scripture is there any endorsement of any homosexual relationship or affirmation of it.

We have the story of David and Jonathan's relationship where David says of Jonathan, "You were very dear to me. Your love for me was wonderful, more wonderful than that of women" (2 Samuel 1:26 NIV), but this is about their "friendship", a very beautiful friendship. In fact, he implies clearly it is non-sexual by the fact this is different or better than a relationship with a woman.

So that is the scripture and the biblical references relating to homosexuality. We can clearly see through scripture that the act of same-sex relationships is not of God, and the same is true for premarital sex in heterosexual relationships. And this has been the consistent understanding of scripture by Christian people in the 2,000 years of its history.

Number 3

However, my purpose here is to be pastoral, as well as understanding the truth of Scripture. For many of us this is a deeply personal issue which may involve members of your family, or involves you yourself – you know what it is to be attracted to members of your own gender.

And so there may be people here who know this tension and this struggle, but let us make one thing clear: no one decides to be homosexual.

Homosexual attraction is not a decision you make, any more than heterosexual attraction is something we decide. If you talk to people who are attracted to their own gender, most of them will tell you that they have been aware of this since puberty. And right from being young, they were aware of these feelings.

The origin of homosexuality, of course, is much debated. Is it nature? Are we born that way? Or is it nurture? Are we made that way by experiences and circumstances?

Those who would come down on the nature side would look for evidence of genetic factors, and there has been a lot of research into that, but from all that I have read, there seems to be no proof of that. Some men are more effeminate than others and some women are more masculine, but that does not in itself equal homosexuality. There are many effeminate men who are completely straight and many women who are more masculine, but they are straight as well. So, although there are theories, and these are speculations, there is no evidence, as far as I am aware, of a homosexual gene being identified.

Regarding nurture, being made that way by experiences and circumstances, the two most popular claims that are made are that a child grows up distant from the same gender – so for a boy, distant maybe emotionally or perhaps physically from his father; a daughter distant from her mother. In due course, this desire to bond with the absent or distant parent takes on a sexual connotation.

It seems to be true. There are many people who are homosexual who would say yes, that was their experience as a child. But there are many children from that same environment who are completely heterosexual.

But there are a number for whom that is not the case, although this is bandied around, and it is a factor in many experiences of many people. The problem with this is that it tends to blacken the character of parents of gay people by this kind of assumption, but it is not universal. It is possibly a factor in the reason why some people are attracted to the same sex.

The other most popular claim is that, as children, they have been interfered with sexually by an older person – boys interfered with by older men, for example – and there was some element of pleasure associated with it. That is the most common factor, but is not universal.

Girls tend to lean more when being abused by a man or by men, so they flee to the security of their own gender. They can't stand being close to a man because of what has been done to them as children.

However, whatever role nature may play or nurture may play, we don't have a simple explanation as to why people have a homosexual orientation. What we have to face is that this is a reality in people's lives, whether we can explain it or not. It is what it is.

For many people, whatever the idea God intended at the beginning, there are people who are gay, and some of them may wish they were not but they have found themselves in the situation, not as a decision but by whatever factors have contributed to that. There is a particular struggle for Christians who find themselves attracted to their own gender.

Talking to gay people, they have helped me to prepare what I'm saying here. These are human beings and just as we would treat a heterosexual who lives with their partner, we are to treat gay people the same way.

A quote from someone who had feelings towards someone of the same sex, but did not act on them:

> "I thought embracing my sexuality would drive me away from God, but it has drawn me that much closer to the throne of grace. There isn't a day goes by when I don't lean on him for guidance."

Love, correction and grace.

And I don't know if that's any different to any other Christian, whether they're gay or straight.

Therefore, it's about the attitude of the heart, very similar to what we said about being single. It's not about marital status, it's about how Christ will fashion his will through us.

It is only when we remember how freely love flows through us that we can truly love each other.

See, homosexual activity is about what people do; homosexual orientation is about who they are.

That is why it is such a deep, a personal and a painful struggle for them.

Number 4

The fourth thing is the strategy by which we need to live in relation to this. We can be clear: homosexual practice is outside of the will of God; homosexual orientation is a fact.

And in some people's lives, whether this can change or not, is a controversial issue.

Some do, and I know people have given testimony to the fact that through various means that orientation has changed significantly. Others testify that they haven't. Some marry in the hope this will provide "a cure". And often it has not changed anything.

I know people who've been prayed for, who've been through extensive counselling. One person told me that he went to confess to a leader in his church that he was struggling with homosexual feelings and they arranged for an exorcism in which to drive out a spirit of homosexuality. But that didn't help him at all.

I think it's best to say change is possible but some live with the fact that "this is who I am".

And I wonder if some of us realise the pain and the agony that people go through struggling with this issue.

How do we come alongside them?

What are the terms about coming alongside them?

What about those who fall?

Let's look again at scripture:

> "If someone is caught in a sin, you who live by the Spirit should restore that person gently. But watch yourself, or you also may be tempted. Carry each other's burdens, and in this way you will fulfil the law of Christ." (Galatians 6:1-2 NIV)

Three things that Paul says here:

1. Restore the person gently. Don't jump on them harshly, but restore them gently; restore them humbly.
2. Watch yourself, says Paul, or you also may be tempted. And if not in this area, in other areas.
3. Carry each other's burdens, and in this way you will fulfil the law of Christ.

Now he addresses this to you who are spiritual.

1. How do you treat homosexuals and lesbians? What defence do you have talking to them?
2. Heterosexuals (men and women) have feelings but don't act as they should, according to the Bible. Why should homosexuals and lesbians?
3. The act of homosexuality and lesbianism is not of God in the Bible, so our approach will always be according to what scripture says. How gentle are we to be with those who disagree? Can we agree to disagree and still be friends?

CHAPTER 8

The sexual revolution and temptation

> "It is God's will that you should be sanctified: that you should avoid sexual immorality; that each of you should learn to control your own body in a way that is holy and honourable, not in passionate lust like the pagans, who do not know God; and that in this matter no one should wrong or take advantage of a brother or sister. The Lord will punish all those who commit such sins, as we told you and warned you before. For God did not call us to be impure, but to live a holy life. Therefore, anyone who rejects this instruction does not reject a human being but God, the very God who gives you his Holy Spirit."
> (1 Thessalonians 4:3-8 NIV)

It should be patently obvious to all of us that we live in a sex-mad culture, that we live in a culture that is indulging itself in every conceivable and inconceivable sexual activity. In fact, it probably would tax your imagination and mine beyond its ability to conceive of a more sexually perverted or immoral society than the one in which we live. Not only is sexual sin tolerated in any form by anyone with anyone else, any time, any place, in any way, but more than just being tolerated, it is advocated, it is promoted, it is marketed through every media means possible. For me to take your valuable time and mine and to clutter your mind and mine with a cataloguing or a chronicling of vices either by way of illustration or statistics, would be to beg the point. It would be like taking ice to Eskimos. You really don't need that.

It is apparent that all of us have been living in a sexual revolution of sorts where it is not uncommon today to find people who call themselves Christians also engaging in every imaginable and unimaginable sexual vice.

It is known that 75 per cent of the Christian young people who come for premarital counselling have already engaged in sexual intercourse. That's in the church. It is apparent that we are living in a sexual revolution. I don't think any of us needs to be informed on that any more than we already are. We live in a culture where there are absolutely no standards or rules about that kind of behaviour.

And the freedom of sexual expression is so demanded that it has become the god that in some ways is ruling over all the other gods in our culture. To put that into an illustrated form, we want to allow people sexual freedom at any cost, even if it means they have to kill the product of that sexual union, right? Therefore, the sexual fulfilment itself is more important than life. We want our sexual freedom even if it means murder of the victim of that freedom.

Looking over at the homosexual community, they wanted their freedom years ago even if it meant the whole population died of AIDS. You see, we've come to the point where we are so totally consumed with sexual behaviour that we literally live with unspeakable, unthinkable consequences.

The pornography and sexual freedom by a man in America called Hugh Hefner has been the guru from the start of this rampant, pornographic life-style. He's the one who really philosophically articulated it. He has been quoted as having written the following words very early in his career as a panderer of vice, which he has done for all these years:

> "Sex is a function of the body, a drive which man shares with animals like eating, drinking, and sleeping. It is a physical demand that must be satisfied. If you don't satisfy it you will have all sorts of neuroses and repression psychoses. Sex is here to stay. Let's forget the prudery that makes us hide from it. Throw away those inhibitions, find a girl who is like-minded, and let yourself go."

Now that is the philosophy of the sexual revolution.

There are several components to it. First of all, sex is simply an animal function. It's no different from eating, drinking or sleeping.

Secondly, it is a physical demand that must be satisfied or you will wind up in a psychiatrist's office because if you don't satisfy it you're going to have all kinds of repressed problems. Thirdly, there are some prudes who would want you not to do that; you've got to ignore them, find a girl who feels the same way, and do it.

We live in that society today. It has reduced itself to bumper stickers: "Do it in the dirt." "Do it here." And the innuendo of all of those kinds of things is sexual. The underlying philosophy of our time is of absolute, sexual freedom to express yourself in any way you want, any time with anyone under any circumstance. The extent of this is absolutely unimaginable and unthinkable.

We might ask ourselves, "Has there ever been a society worse than this?" May I be so bold as to answer the question by saying yes! Hugh Hefner could have sold his same philosophy in Thessalonica. Hugh Hefner could have sold his same philosophy in Corinth. He could have sold it to Greek culture in the Roman world.

And somebody with another name did, or somebodies with a lot of other names did, because in the Roman world at the time that Paul wrote 1 Thessalonians, there was a sexual revolution which, if anything, surpassed the one we are now living through.

They had experienced a sexual revolution which included homosexuality, which included paedophilia (homosexual sex with boys), which included effeminate transvestitism (men dressing up like women), which included every form of fornication and sexual perversion. It was true in the Roman world. And unlike today, there wasn't any preliminary Christian culture to act as a sort of barrier along the way. Consequently, they had their venereal epidemics, as we do, and all the rest of the things that are attendant upon a fornicating society.

Now the Greek language has an immense capacity to articulate because of the vastness of its vocabulary and the specificity of its words. So, I pulled out a few of the Greek words that would help you get a feeling for the kind of culture to which Paul writes here.

The Greek language is amply capable of cataloguing all kinds of deviant sexual sins and there are varying words that make that very clear.

Here is quick survey which will help. And I'm only dealing with the heterosexual sins at this point.

1 Thessalonians 4:3-8

The first word to look at is porn. Porn literally means "the purchasable one", the one you buy, the harlot, the whore, the prostitute. They had that word because they had that. In the society in which Paul lived and to which he penned this letter and in which he founded churches under the power of the Holy Spirit, there was prostitution. They had that in Thessalonica. They had a sort of free-sex mentality because prostitution was legal. Women could be bought.

A second word to keep in mind in the Greek language is a form of the first word, *pernmi*, and it sums up the filthy business of making a living by prostitution. It encompasses the prostitution, the pimping, the whole thing that goes on with that entire business. So they not only had the individual woman who could be bought, who sold herself, but they had the big business – the stable, if you will, of prostitutes.

Then there's the Greek word *puloke*. *Puloke* means "concubine". A concubine was a slave whose primary function was to fulfil sexual desire. Literally, you purchased the concubine, you added her to your fold of concubines, and you used her for sexual pleasure. That, too, was legal. That, too, was rampant in the Roman world. So there was the one-time woman you purchased and the whole business of prostitution, and then there was the long-term purchased woman, the concubine, the slave for sexual pleasure.

And then there was another word, *eteri*. This was different from the concubine; you didn't buy this woman. This was a friend. Typically, men and women had these kinds of friends outside their marriage. By the way, your wife was primarily to take care of the house, cook the meals, keep the clothes clean, and watch the children. The wife was not primarily the sexual partner. Sexual fulfilment was found in the one-time enterprise of a prostitute, the long-term responsibility of a concubine, or the now-and-then relationship with this friend who was both an intellectual friend as well as a sexual partner.

There was another word, *moichos*. This refers to the adulterer or the adulteress. You could have a sexual relationship with a prostitute on an occasional basis which you purchased, you could own a concubine or more concubines for sexual pleasure, you could have mistresses, or, reversing the situation, mistresses would have men (for every man who commits sexual sin there is a partner, obviously), there was the friend you didn't buy, the mutual agreement, sort of casual sex with someone you knew very well. And then there was *moichos*, an adulterer or adulteress. This was having sex with somebody else's spouse. And it was all going on, all of it, filling up the Thessalonian culture, as well as the Corinthian culture, as well as the whole Roman culture.

Unmarried young men were also allowed to have intercourse with mistresses. They were encouraged to have intercourse with mistresses, but those mistresses could not be daughters of families that had full citizenship in the Roman Empire. Those were considered significant families and these young men were not to touch those girls. But they could engage themselves with prostitutes and they could engage themselves with mistresses whose parents were not full citizens of the Roman Empire.

Now you could go one step beyond that and add temple prostitutes. The Babylonian, cultic, mystery religions that filtered all the way down into the time of the apostle Paul and were the mythological religions of that time, advocated prostitution. Why? Because they taught that if you had relationships with a priestess – prostitute – you were communing with the deity she represented. The way to get in touch with the deity was by a sexual liaison with a priestess. The temple in Corinth, for example, had 3,000 temple prostitutes to get people in contact with the deity (by the way, a very popular and convenient form of religion). But you can see by that that it was condoned. Today, at least in America, religious prostitution is still a crime.

But they had it all. Now you add to that homosexuality, paedophilia, whatever other kinds of deviant things were going on, and that was the culture in which Paul lived and to which he wrote. If you think it's bad today, you probably would have found it worse then. The difference would have been media. You wouldn't have been exposed to it sort involuntarily to the degree that you are today, to the point now where young people think there's nothing wrong with it at all, even going so far as some Christian couples who think that because they're engaged they can engage in anything they choose. We have been so desensitised to this sin, but so had they in Paul's day.

Sexual sin then was common. Sexual sin was tolerated. Sexual sin was customary, just as today and maybe even more so. Now why is that important? It's important because of this: Paul went in to Thessalonica with his two friends Timothy and Silas. They went there to preach the gospel. They went there to found a church. In founding that church, they were rescuing people out of this pornographic culture. Obviously, these people had lived a pagan lifestyle. They had a former religion in which they engaged in sexual intercourse with temple prostitutes. They probably were involved with concubinage. They no doubt had their *eteri*, their mistresses. They perhaps had their harlots and their whores.

And now all of a sudden, they come to the knowledge of Jesus Christ. And there's this little island of salvation in a sea of paganism. And Paul is very concerned about them because he knows that old habits act as a very strong temptation to the new life. You don't forget those habits easily, if at all. And the apostle knew that this relatively new group of Christians, only months old in the Lord (he only preached three Sabbaths in the synagogue, a few weeks after that to the Gentiles, and then he was gone a few months before he wrote back to them the first letter to the Thessalonians), it's only a few months since they were saved. He knows the pull of those old habits and he knows the push of that wicked culture is going to make this a major problem.

And so, finally he comes to chapter four, which is his real purpose in writing. The first three chapters he's just been defending his own integrity and the integrity of his ministry and affirming the integrity of the church. It's all been a discussion about himself, his ministry, and the church. It's all foundation. Now here's what he really wants to talk about. He wants to reiterate the commands of Christian living. He wants them to walk as they ought to walk so to please God. He wants them to excel still more and keep the commandments he gave them by the authority of the Lord Jesus. And he starts off in verse 3 all the way to the end of chapter 5 with those commands. He says, "You know what commandments we gave you." Verse 1: "You already received the instruction. You know what we've said." This is only a reminder. Verse 6 at the end: "We told you before and solemnly warned you."

Now it's a good thing to note here, folks, Paul went in, preached the gospel, led these people to Christ and then, believe me, he fulfilled the great commission, which is not only to go and not only to baptise – that is to get them saved – but "Teaching them to observe all things whatsoever I have commanded you" (Matthew 28:20 KJV). So he gave them principles of holy living.

But he's been gone a few months. He knows the pull and the push: the pull of old habits, the push of a godless, sexually deviated culture. And he is concerned and he wants to share this with them. If he had his choice he would go and tell them face to face, right? Look back in 1 Thessalonians 2:17-18. He says he was hindered, he couldn't get there, so he has to write. So starting in chapter 2, he unfolds these exhortations. Number one on the list is a call to sexual purity. That is the first issue. Why? Because the pagan society was so wretched, that was the compelling sin. Why do you think when the apostle Paul writes about the standards for leadership in the church he starts with being above reproach, being a one-woman man? Because that was the dominating cultural milieu, sexual deviation. It's just like today.

Paul then is building on what he had already told them. And he's going to clarify it and he's going to drive it home. The first subject on the list: sexual sin. Why? Major problem, major issue; the desire is so strong, the temptation is so compelling, the past was so sinful, the society was so corrupt. Paul knows this is a major issue. By the way, no shame was attached to premarital intercourse. No shame was attached to extramarital intercourse. This had been their lifestyle. The Thessalonian culture was famous for sexual vice.

But Paul says, "In spite of cultural habits, in spite of your old patterns, the Lord does not tolerate sexual sin." The church can't live like the world. It doesn't matter how the world lives. Just because the world sinks deeper and deeper and deeper into the muck, doesn't mean we sink with it. Just because they lower their standards lower and lower and lower, doesn't mean we lower ours a little bit. This is not a relative morality; this is an absolute standard. It doesn't change. It doesn't fluctuate. All forms of sexual gratification may be indulged in by a society but not the church, not Christians.

Now you might ask, "Well, were there some specific people or groups or specific sins that the Thessalonians were committing?" Paul doesn't mention any, not like 1 Corinthians where he writes about the same issue and mentions one guy who was having a sexual relationship with his father's wife, his step-mother. We don't know of any particulars but we can be very sure that because this is at the top of his list of exhortations as he begins the exhortative section, that this was the major problem. And I would believe that it is preventative rather than some specific rebuke or he would have perhaps zeroed in on someone.

Points for discussion are covered in the following chapter.

CHAPTER 9

Biblical questions and answers

> "It is God's will that you should be sanctified: that you should avoid sexual immorality; that each of you should learn to control your own body in a way that is holy and honourable, not in passionate lust like the pagans, who do not know God; and that in this matter no one should wrong or take advantage of a brother or sister. The Lord will punish all those who commit such sins, as we told you and warned you before. For God did not call us to be impure, but to live a holy life. Therefore, anyone who rejects this instruction does not reject a human being but God, the very God who gives you his Holy Spirit."
> (1 Thessalonians 4:3-8 NIV)

As we come to this passage I'm going to ask three questions and these three questions will give us a very clear understanding of the issue.

Discussion Questions

1. What does God require?
2. How can I fulfil it?
3. Why should I?

Those questions will unfold the deep, direct, powerful meaning of this text.

What does God require in the area of sexual behaviour?

Verse 3 says that it is the will of God that you should be sanctified; that you abstain from sexual immorality. It's pretty clear, isn't it? Just to make sure nobody finds an escape hatch here, let's look more closely at it. "It is the will of God."

It always amazes me how many people are stumbling around trying to find the will of God. You notice that? "It is the will of God." You want to walk and please God? You want to excel still more? You want to do what God wants you to do? Well then, this is it. And since all Christians have holy longings, since all Christians have holy aspirations, since all Christians to some degree want to do what's right, because that's what the new nature does, then Paul assumes his readers are desirous of doing God's will and all they need to know is what it is. He assumes – Romans 7 – that you're going to desire to do what's right even though we don't always do it. So he says this is the will of God.

This is not my opinion. This is not some human system. This is God's will. And again I say I am constantly amazed at how many people struggle to know God's will. I really do believe that most of the problems – well, I could say it simply, all of the problems – that people have are strictly a result of not doing God's will. Would you agree to that? I mean, if you're in the middle of God's will, that's not a problem. You may have trouble in this world but you'll be riding across the top of it. If people would just know God's will it would be the elimination of all the difficulties in life, not by all positive circumstances but by all positive attitudes under the grace of Christ.

Now what is God's will? I can give it to you very quickly. God's will is that you be saved. And I've said this before, "By his will he begot you" (see James 1:18). God wants you to be saved.

Secondly, he wants you to sacrifice. What do we mean by that? "To offer your bodies as a living sacrifice, holy and pleasing to God" (Romans 12:1 NIV). God wants you to yield up yourself to him. He wants you to be saved and he wants you to make the sacrifice of yourself.

He wants you to be Spirit-controlled. "Do not be unwise, but understand what the will of the Lord is. Do not be drunk with wine . . . but be filled with the Spirit" (Ephesians 5:17-18 NKJV). God's will is that you be Spirit-controlled. God's will is that you be saved. God's will is that you make the sacrifice of your body continually to Christ.

God's will is also that you be satisfied. "In every thing give thanks: for this is the will of God in Christ Jesus concerning you" (1 Thessalonians 5:18 KJV). Be satisfied. God's will is that you be satisfied. God's will is that you be submissive. Submit yourselves to all those in authority (1 Peter 2:13), that's the will of God. God's will is that you suffer. It is the will of God that you suffer awhile for the cause of the gospel (1 Peter 3:17). God's will is that you supplicate, or pray (1 John 5:14-15). All of that is God's will.

Now you show me a person who is saved, continually yielding over their body as a living sacrifice, Spirit-controlled, satisfied, submissive, suffering for the sake of the gospel, supplicating or taking their needs to the Lord according to his will, knowing that he hears and will answer, and I'll show you a person who is victorious, right? That's not the kind of person who needs to go to the Christian therapist.

But there's one other thing and it sort of gobbles up all the rest. It's right here. This is the will of God: your sanctification. What does it mean by that? What does sanctification mean? The word *hagiasmos* means separate, apart, set apart, holy. It simply means this: to be set apart from sin to God. God's will is that you be set apart from sin to God – it's a very simple concept. Now that's a process, the process of becoming holy. That's God's will. He wants you to become holy – this is his will.

By the way, that little phrase "this is the will of God, your sanctification" (ESV) could really be the sort of umbrella to cover the rest of the book because every other principle that is given and every other exhortation is an element of sanctification. So there's a sense in which the first part of verse 3 sort of just covers it all. God's will is that you be set apart unto him in a process of becoming holy from sin towards God and here's how, and all the rest of the whole book will tell you how. But principle number one, look at it, verse 3: "that you abstain from sexual immorality" (ESV). That's the first principle of a sanctified life. If you're not covering this principle in your life, the rest in some ways is a moot point. This is where we start. We start with a holy life.

Back in chapter 3 verse 13, what was Paul's great prayer? That your hearts would be blameless in holiness before God. God wants you holy. God wants you separated. God wants you set apart from sin to him; separation from all that is wicked, all that is filthy, all that is evil, all that is impure, all that is fleshly, all that is sinful. That's the general concept. That's the general introduction to the whole section.

You see, when you were saved you were saved unto sanctification. Paul says in Romans 6:19 and Romans 6:22, "You used to be the slaves of sin." Then he says, "You're now the slaves of righteousness which results in sanctification." The process of becoming holy is a direct result of salvation. You were saved and the process of becoming holy began and, step one, abstain from immorality. Simple.

What does that mean? Stay away from sexual sin. Now young people always want to say, "How far away? How far away do I have to stay?" Which means, "How far can I go and still be okay?" Is it okay to hold hands and hug each other? Is it okay to kiss? Is it okay to touch each other? Is it okay to go beyond that as long you don't do the very act? What can I do? Is it okay if we're engaged? Is it okay if we've decided that somewhere down the road we are going to get married? How far can I go?"

That isn't even the right question. That question betrays a sinful heart. The question isn't how far can I go and get away with it. The question is, how can I be sanctified, separated from sin and holy unto God?

How can I conduct my physical relationships so that I am holy, separated from sin?

As you begin to play with the emotions that God has designed to lead to consummation and intercourse, you begin to allow your mind to move into the area of thinking about that. You are in sin because if a man in his mind commits adultery, in God's eyes, the sin has been committed, right? If a woman commits it in the mind, it's been committed before God because he sees the mind.

You have to stop short of the impure thought, the impure motive, the lustful passion. The question isn't how far can I go and still be okay? The question is how can I be holy, how can I be utterly separated from sin, how can I be totally pure, completely holy unto God, pleasing him? How can I excel still more? How can I be more excellent? Not how can I drift a little bit the other way and just get on the edge?

As I said, every imaginable and every unimaginable form of sexual vice was running loose in Thessalonica, as it is in our society, and there were Christians who were weak, just as there are Christians today who are weak. There were Christians who were sort of witless and ignorant about things and a bit naive, maybe wilfully. There were Christians who were shallow. There were some who, because of former lifestyle or because of exposure to pornographic experiences, had had their lusts pandered and pandered and pandered, like people who go to the movies all the time or read dirty magazines or listen to the kind of music which literally fuels the fire of their own lusts. They had them then just like there are people today like that. And they would be strongly pulled towards sexual sin. It would have been easy for them to fall into it, and that was Paul's concern.

Sometimes some of us think, "Well I don't have those pulls. I didn't have an adulterous life before I was converted. I didn't fornicate before I was converted." Or "I got married as a virgin and I don't go to those kinds of movies." But I'll tell you right now, you live in a society that is lowering and lowering and lowering the resistance continuously by overexposing us to all of this and laughing at it and treating it as triviality so that we no longer think anything of it. We can see a television show where a prostitute is a comedic character and we can laugh about that because our senses have been so totally dulled to it. And as that gets lowered and lowered and lowered, even though we haven't had a wide exposure to that kind of behaviour, we can become more susceptible to that kind of a temptation because of our resistance being broken down.

Paul knew that reality. And so he makes a very simple, direct command. It is not complicated at all. He says, "Abstain from immorality." What does the word "abstain" mean? *Apechomai*, complete abstinence, stay away from it all together. You say, "What is sexual immorality?" Any act that violates the principles of God's Word; any thought that violates the principle of God's Word leading to that act. Whatever relationship you have with someone of the opposite sex other than your spouse, it had better not include any act or thought designed to culminate in sexual intercourse. I don't care whether you're engaged to them, or whether you're committed, or whatever that might mean – God says total abstinence.

What is immorality? Immorality is the word *porneia*. It simply means illicit sexual behaviour. It's a broad word. It covers all forms of sexual sin. Anything other than a monogamous relationship in a marriage, anything other than husband and wife, any other sexual relationship to any degree is pornographic by God's standard. Now God isn't down on sex (Hebrews 13). God invented it to start with for man's pleasure; it even says so in the Old Testament. Some people say, "Well it's just for procreation, it's just for having children." No, because even the Old Testament talks about one of the patriarchs sporting with his wife. Now I'm not going to go into a Hebrew definition of sporting, you can use your imagination. But the idea was it was for pure pleasure.

Now you come to Hebrews 13:4 which says, "Marriage is honourable among all, and the bed undefiled" (NKJV). A marriage bed is undefiled; you can't defile a marriage bed. Two people who are married in bed, that is undefiled; the full expression of sexual pleasure there is by God's design. But fornicators and adulterers, God will judge. God draws the line at that point. The marriage bed, that's where the line is drawn. Any bed other than a marriage bed, God will judge.

Now looking at 1 Thessalonians, there were very likely critics who were accusing Paul of being like the rest of the false teachers, charlatans, frauds and people who came seeking sexual favours from women followers. It was pretty typical of ancient times that these phony philosophers and religious leaders would come and they would seek women around them and their goal was to get prestige, to get some power, to make some money and to get sexual favours from women followers. That was pretty typical. By the way, if you think that's old, you better think again. That's going on even today. There are all kinds of religious charlatans who are in it for the sexual favours today, as scandals of our own time have revealed. They were accusing Paul of seeking sexual favours from women, so when he says this, that God's standard is total abstinence, he not only gives them a command but he puts his own life on the line as subscribing to that very thing as well.

His attitude is very simple: total abstinence. God has designed sex for the marriage bed alone. In Ephesians 5:3 Paul wrote, "Sexual immorality and all impurity or covetousness must not even be named among you, as is proper among saints" (ESV). No kind of immorality, *porneia* again, sexual sin, no kind of impurity should ever be named among you because you are saints – *hagios* – same word, you are set apart, you're holy, you're in the process of becoming like God. No kind of sexual sin should ever be so much as named among you. It is utterly inconsistent with sanctification.

In Colossians Paul says very much the same thing: "Your life is hid with Christ in God" (Colossians 3:3 KJV). You belong to God, you're in a process of sanctification. Consider then the members of your earthly body as dead, or desensitised, insensitive, unresponsive to immorality, impurity, passion and evil desire – words with sexual significance. You're a Christian. "Your life is hid with Christ in God." You're headed for glory. You can't be responding to that.

Now the command is very, very, clear: total abstinence from any sexual relationship outside the marriage bed. And I'll promise you that's God's design not to make your life unhappy but to make your marriage all the bliss that God could possibly intend it to be. Violate it and you will throw into your marriage a component that may result in a disastrous or divorced union. God has given his Word; that's the basic command.

How am I supposed to fulfil that? How do I control myself?

Although few Christians accept the basic goodness of man, we do worse and accept the basic goodness of ourselves. We are vulnerable to the sins of the flesh as we have seen repeatedly among Christian leaders and laity alike. We compete with the world's hyper-sexuality, saying that good sex will make a good marriage when it is commitment, communication and sacrifice that come first. By implying that sex is the key to marriage, we teach our unmarried youth to focus on the physical in their relationships with the opposite gender. We encourage technique instead of commitment. And we prepare all for disappointment in marriage because sex is not meant to be the ultimate satisfaction.

They say, "Marriage is two people joining together with all their faults. How can we expect total bliss from that?" We have embraced *eros* instead of *agape* love. And no Greek word could better describe the sexual revolution than *eros*. The advocates of this sexual freedom would unashamedly agree. This is the heart of the problem because *eros* is love that desires to have or possess, and so is basically self-centred. A person controlled by *eros* enters a relationship, if there is a relationship at all, to seize what he desires. The Christian version of this is the adoption of self-actualising psychology which demands self-fulfilment in marriage in place of sacrifice.

The church has literally imbibed this. And when you go back and look at the roots of it all, you really could start with Charles Darwin. Once the thinking of Charles Darwin, which I believe was certainly spawned by Satan, invaded the world and said, "We are not the creatures of God, we are simply the products of chance," then all morality was questionable. If we are nothing but the result of a collection of atoms that occurred sometime in the past, or something that crawled out of some primeval ooze somewhere, then there is no real morality. Charles Darwin influenced people like Karl Marx, who took Darwinian evolution to its logical extreme politically. And he influenced people like Sigmund Freud who took Darwinian evolution to its extreme in terms of psychology and personal behaviour. They influenced people like Friedrich Nietzsche, who decided that really there was no God, God was dead, family life was unimportant. All that was important was pleasure and fulfilment.

They influenced philosophers like Bertrand Russell who mocked all Christian values, and along came people influenced by them: Margaret Sanger, who founded Planned Parenthood; Ernest Hemingway, probably the most classically famous hedonist in western culture; Havelock Ellis; Margaret Mead; Alfred Kinsey; Masters and Johnson; Hugh Hefner. And they all flow out of that same basic line of philosophical thinking. What you have is a sexual revolution produced by atheistic, hedonistic, pleasure-mad, anti-family, pornographic, perverted people. It starts, as it were, supposedly in the environs of science and philosophy; it ends up in behaviour. Mix that kind of behaviour with alcohol and drugs and you have the American culture. And what is so frightening about it is that the church doesn't seem to be aware of what's happening and it jumps on the self-fulfilling, feeling-good bandwagon, unwittingly capitulating to the philosophy of atheists and evolutionists.

And I guess we would have to say that in Paul's time the kind of behaviour that existed there would have been as bad and, as I said earlier, maybe worse. There was no shame attached to immoral behaviour at all in Paul's time. No shame attached to any sexual conduct at all. There was, in that society, a plethora of prostitutes, concubines, mistresses, homosexuals, paedophiles, transvestites, temple harlots, adulterers and adulteresses, and they abounded in that culture. In fact, it was from that very mass of people that the churches were plucked. Paul says to the Corinthians, "And such were some of you." What? "Fornicators, adulterers, homosexuals, effeminates."

Now keep in mind that as Paul is writing back to the Thessalonians, he's writing to some people who have only been Christians a few months. They're in every sense baby Christians. He spent but a few weeks there in the Jewish synagogue, a few weeks more, no doubt, evangelising Gentiles. He's been gone a few months and is now writing back, deeply concerned that these people are not falling victim to the pull of their old habits and the pressure of that ungodly, immoral culture. When he finally in chapter 4 gets to what he really wants to say, the first thing on his list is this matter of immorality. The dominating idolatry of their day was sexual immorality, as it is of our day.

Now what is Paul's word to a people who are in the muck of that kind of society? Let your body control the situation, not the situation control your body. Live a godly life.

CHAPTER 10

The danger of the media and what you watch

Trying to understand the power and purpose of the kingdom of the media

The actor Arnold Schwarzenegger can spend $120 million on a two-hour movie and make $200 million.

This why the television is so dangerous and so powerful, and why the radio is so effective.

The nature of the media.

Some principles I want us to look at.

The first one is that there's nothing on earth as powerful as the human will. There is nothing more powerful than that. As a matter of fact, the human will is so powerful that God himself does not control it. We do remember that there's one thing that God does not control on Earth and that's the human will. Why? Because the very nature of will implies self-control. God gave you the power of "will".

Number two, the will controls the destiny of man. Your will is the agency of God's kingdom administration. When God established his kingdom on earth, he wanted it to be administered through your will. The problem is, your will is yours. The most dangerous gift God ever gave man was a "will".

And the most precious gift God gave you is the same power and the ability to choose. So God wanted you to use your will for his will.

Number three, the seed of the will is the conscious and the subconscious mind. That's where things will live, it lives in the heart (thinking).

Your heart is your subconscious mind, and your subconscious mind is the seat of control for your life. You've got two minds: you've got a conscious mind and a subconscious mind. So you've got a mind that is always conscious but then you've got a mind beneath that, that is not always conscious but it's deeper and more important than your conscious mind. And your conscious mind feeds your subconscious mind information. And the more your conscious mind hears something, it feeds into the subconscious mind.

That is why repetition and "habitual sin" is dangerous. Repetition constantly goes to your conscious mind. But the more your conscious mind hears something, it begins to deposit it or, to use a technical term, it downloads it to your subconscious mind.

If it's in your conscious mind it remains safe, but then once repetition happens, it gets into your subconscious mind. Once it gets there, then you are in trouble. Why? Because the mind is the centre of thought and it holds the key to life.

Proverbs 23:7 says, "As [a man] thinketh in his heart, so is he" (KJV).

There are two things to look at here: there's thinking and there's a heart thing. "Heart" here is a Hebrew word referring to the subconscious mind.

Solomon says you are whatever is in your subconscious mind. Your subconscious mind is your heart. Whoever controls your heart controls your life. That is why, if you are watching distasteful things like pornography, or listening to sexual language, it will eventually enter your subconscious mind, which becomes dangerous – it will control you! Whoever can get enough information into your subconscious mind will control you because as a man thinks in his heart, that's the man.

So if you want to control the man, all you've got to do is control his heart.

And how do you control his heart?

First, you work on the conscious mind and you keep repeating, repeating and repeating until the conscious mind deposits it in the heart. And now you're in trouble. That is why some of you have problems with battles or things you try to change and you can't change them. Old habits that you were keeping for the last twenty years and now you want to change are just tough to change. Young people, that is why God tells you to stay away from evil things. If you keep watching pornography, you keep reading dirty books, you keep listening to bad stories or dirty jokes. And if you keep listening – not the first time you see it, it doesn't bother you – but if you keep seeing it, it becomes downloaded.

Then once something is downloaded on your "hard drive", what happens even when you are not conscious of it, is it is still running and all you've got to do is press the right button and you see all the pictures in colour.

> "Consider carefully what you hear . . . With the measure you use, it will be measured to you – and even more." (Mark 4:24 NIV)

If you don't control what comes into your conscious mind, it will soon become a part of your subconscious mind and it's in your heart

> "Out of the abundance of the heart the mouth speaketh." (Matthew 12:34 KJV)

The heart comes with the issues of life. And Jesus said from murders and adultery. He said they are coming from the heart. The mind is defined as the heart. It determines the future and destiny of a man.

I guess what I'm saying is you are a sum total of the choices you make every day. And whatever you decide to hear and see and listen to constantly will become your future. You become what you continually hear; you become what you continually see. That's as simple as life is. Some of you are still plagued with habits that you've been trying to break. And I know I've been dealing with people in counselling who've been born again for 20 years who are still struggling, who downloaded some stuff that is still there.

How do you clean a hard-drive of stuff that's been downloaded? Well, that's a tough thing to do. Sometimes you've got to buy a whole new computer.

What you've got to do is buy another programme that literally cleans it out. That's what the Holy Ghost is: God's software. Glory hallelujah. And the material is the Word of God. You're supposed to constantly keep hearing the Word of God until it drowns out what was there for 20 years. That's the only way to do it.

Now it's really a battle for the soul. The mind is the centre of the soul. What is the soul? The soul is an integration of three parts: the mind, the will and the emotions.

What is your mind, your will, your emotions?

Your feelings are in your soul. Your decision-making power is in your soul. And your mind, your thinking bank, is in your soul (mind, emotions and will) that makes your soul the most important part of your life.

Let me explain why the battle in life is for the soul of man.

The Bible says, "He that winneth souls is wise" (Proverbs 11:30 KJV).

Now why don't you just say that? See, reading a body is no problem. Even winning a spirit is easy. You get born again in a second. But winning your soul is a tough job.

My job as a teacher and a communicator is to work on your soul. I am after your soul. I want to win your soul. I've already won your body because you're here, reading this book, and I've already won your spirit because you want to find God, but winning your soul is a tougher job.

So the battle is for what? Your soul, the soul of the people, the soul of the nation, the soul of your children, the soul of your spouse, the soul of your entire job. Your soul is in trouble. The attack is against your soul.

The soul is the first component of media created by God.

Why is the soul the first component of media? You've got to think about this. The soul is the mediator between the spirit and the body. The soul is the most dangerous part of your life. As a matter of fact, your spirit is not your problem. The devil is not after your body, or spirit.

But there's a key component that he can still manipulate: soul (mind, emotions and will).

What does the soul do?

The soul receives from the senses. In other words, hearing, tasting, seeing, touching and feeling all come to the senses. But they all go to the soul. They go to your mind, your will and your emotions. So whatever you see, touch, taste, feel or hear goes to your soul.

Now if your soul takes it and deposits it into you, which is your spirit, then you've got to make sure, regulate what the soul is picking up from the senses.

That's why Jesus said, "Take heed what you hear" (Mark 4:24 NKJV). He means be selective. Regulate your hearing or seeing; choose what you want to listen to. It could mess up your whole life. Your soul receives from the senses and the person, your spirit, but here's the other side: the Spirit reveals through the soul to the body.

The Bible says, "Faith comes by hearing", and you hear through what? The body. The soul takes it, believes it and gives it to the spirit; not a spirit receives and conceives it. If the Spirit of God is in you, the Spirit of God says, no, that is not righteous information.

The Bible says do not walk in the flesh but "walk in the Spirit, and you shall not fulfil the lust of the flesh" (Galatians 5:6 NKJV).

The first words of Jesus in his public ministry, Matthew 4:17 says, "Jesus began to preach, 'Repent . . . '" The word "repent" means to change your mind. Where's your mind? In your soul. His first attention was given to the soul. If I can get your soul changed, he says, then the kingdom can come from heaven on earth.

God is battling for your soul. So is Satan. That's my point. Satan and God really are not after your body, even though that's important for the earth. They're really after your soul because whoever controls your soul controls you. We forgot where the battle is. We've become so spiritual, that sometimes we have actually invented demons that don't exist. Are we fighting things that aren't there?

Jesus Christ is called the mediator between God and man. The Bible says there's only one medium between God and man and that is Jesus. Feed your soul with the Word of God.

Discussion Questions

1. What am I feeding to my soul (mind, emotions and will)?

2. Am I addicted to pornography?

3. Do I pretend to others that I am righteous, but do things I shouldn't do?

4. Am I accountable to someone?

5. Do I watch movies with sex, abusive language, extreme violence?

CHAPTER 11

How to choose the right person to avoid later regrets or divorce

According to recent statistics, 42 per cent of marriages in England and Wales end in divorce.

The latest statistics show that 108,421 couples divorced in 2019. Of these, 107,599 were opposite-sex couples, and 822 were same-sex couples – double the number of same-sex divorces in 2018 (428 couples). Of these same-sex divorces, 72 per cent were between female couples.

I've done very extensive research and a lot of teaching in the area of divorce and marriage. Divorce is not only a major problem today, but it was a major problem 2,000 years ago and as old as the Fall.

Moses was the first person that we know in history to do something officially about marital disintegration. Moses developed a legislation, introduced a bill in his constitutional costs of leading a nation of over 1 million people.

Of course, he had to deal with these social problems and he developed a bill that he introduced among the people to prevent people from destroying each other. And that's why he introduced the bill of divorcement.

The bill of divorcement meant that a man in those days – of course women were unlikely to have many rights – man was the one to initiate this very traumatic, horrifying experience of officially separating a union.

And so in Matthew 19:1-11, we find that the Pharisees and Scribes approached Jesus and asked him about his view of divorce. Jesus answered the question, but he ignored the issue in the sense that he really didn't deal with divorce, rather the source behind it.

Jesus saw divorce as a symptom. A problem that needs dealing with is the cause. A symptom has to do with a sign. So divorce is a sign that something else is wrong.

It's like a pain in the body. When there's a pain in your body, the pain is not the problem. The pain is an indication that there is a problem.

In fact, your body was created by God to be such a unique machine, that whenever something was wrong with your body, the neurological system, which is your nervous apparatus, will communicate to your brain that something is wrong somewhere. And the neurological impulses send the signal of that problem to the brain; the brain then sends a signal back to that area and tells the area to emit a signal that there's a problem there. The signal that the area emits is called "pain".

So when you feel the pain, the pain is not the problem. The pain is your neurological system telling your whole body that something's wrong in that location. And then you can act on and pursue the problem. Divorce is the same way. The fact that there are so many problems in our families and the disintegration of marriages and broken homes is not the problem. The problem is that something else is wrong and divorce is the symptom. That's why divorce is so painful.

The word "divorce" is from the Greek word *apostasies*. It is a big word but it simply means "to defect". So to divorce a person means you have defected. Defection is used in military terms when a person has committed themselves to fight for an army or a cause. When you join the armed forces of a country, you have committed yourself to fight for that country. Whenever you join an army, you have committed yourself not to live but to die. Armies are not motivated by life. Armies are motivated by death. In other words, when you join an army, they don't guarantee you're going to survive if you fight in a war. They can guarantee you that you might die. Now, if you survive, then they say you are a hero.

When you join an army, you've committed yourself to death. Well, the word used for divorce is the same word that is used for the military.

And that is when you walk down an aisle and you commit yourself to another person: the man to the woman and the woman to the man.

You're not committing yourself to life – that's why marriages don't work, because we keep getting married for life – you are joining yourself to someone just like you join yourself to an army, and you are deciding that the only way you will be separated is by death.

Now when you join an army and you decide with your brothers and your colleagues that you've had enough, the enemy is too strong, that the weapons they have are too awesome and you've become afraid, intimidated by the environment, you've become so frightened by the reality that you say to your colleagues, "I am no longer going to stay with you. I'm going to turn back. I'm going back home to be a civilian." The army calls that "defection". The Greek word is divorce.

What happens when a soldier defects? Court Marshall. If a soldier has turned their back, the only thing a defector deserves in the military is death. Why? Because the only thing that's supposed to separate you from your colleagues is death.

That's the spirit of defections.

I give you my whole life.

I give you my body.

I give you my emotions.

I give you my entire future.

I give you everything and you are going to turn your back on it.

Defection.

Here's why. When a person dies, they are taken to the morgue. They're placed in a box. You have a funeral. Everybody wears black. You go to this place called a church. You have a ceremony. You take them to the cemetery. You put them in a hole. You put dirt on them.

That is closure.

But divorce, it's worse because when you get a divorce, if the marriage is finished you bury it. You walk away but then there's resurrection again. That's why it's worse than death because the person keeps coming back. You stand on the Tube. You stand at the bus stop. There they are. The Bible tells us in Malachi 2:16 that God hates divorce.

So then we find the question being asked of Jesus:

"Some Pharisees came to [Jesus] to test him. They asked, 'Is it lawful for a man to divorce his wife for any and every reason?'" (Matthew 19:3 NIV)

His response:

"Haven't you read . . . that at the beginning the Creator 'made them male and female,' and said, 'For this reason a man will leave his father and mother and be united to his wife, and the two will become one flesh'? So, they are no longer two, but one flesh. Therefore, what God has joined together, let no one separate." (Matthew 19:4-6 NIV)

Discussion Questions

1. How do you pray that the Lord will direct you to the right person?

2. Do you believe the person you choose to date will be your life long Christian partner?

3. How committed are you to being with someone for life?

4. What do you know about the person you want marry?

5. Is external attraction everything?

CONCLUSION

God forgives.

No matter what your past, God can make you spiritually pure in his eyes. Old things pass away, and all things become new! That's how the blood of Jesus Christ works, to wash away sin. To restore and cleanse and renew your mind.

Prayer . . .

Dear Lord,

I know I have sinned and been involved with things of a sexual nature. I ask for your forgiveness and strength that I won't get involved with anything that is abhorrent to you. So, help me in these areas until such time I find the right partner. Amen.